# FÜTCHI PERF

'fyooCHee purf'

PRODUCTION ASSIST: JORDAN SHIVELEY
DESIGN: KEVIN CZAP

UNCIVILIZED BOOKS
P. O. BOX 6534
MINNEAPOLIS, MN 55406
USA
UNCIVILIZEDBOOKS.COM

FIRST EDITION, OCTOBER 2017
10 9 8 7 6 5 4 3 2 1
ISBN 978-1-941250-21 -1

DISTRIBUTED TO THE TRADE BY:
CONSORTIUM BOOK SALES & DISTRIBUTION, LLC.
34 THIRTEENTH AVENUE NE,
SUITE 101
MINNEAPOLIS, MN 55413-1007
CBSD.COM
ORDERS: (800) 283-3572

PRINTED IN CHINA

# FÜTCHI PERF

## KEVIN CZAP

UNCIVILIZED BOOKS, PUBLISHER

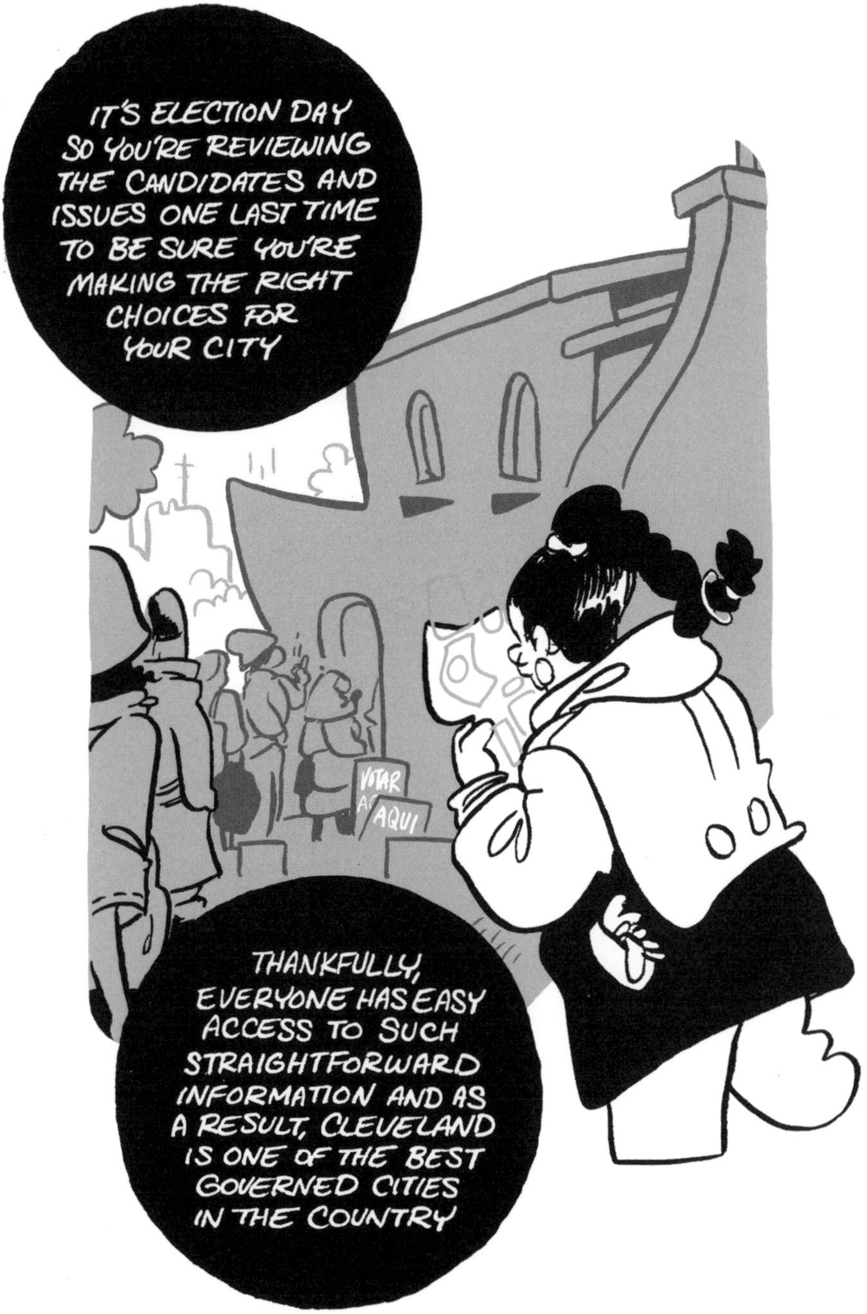
IT'S ELECTION DAY SO YOU'RE REVIEWING THE CANDIDATES AND ISSUES ONE LAST TIME TO BE SURE YOU'RE MAKING THE RIGHT CHOICES FOR YOUR CITY
VOTAR AQUI
THANKFULLY, EVERYONE HAS EASY ACCESS TO SUCH STRAIGHTFORWARD INFORMATION AND AS A RESULT, CLEVELAND IS ONE OF THE BEST GOVERNED CITIES IN THE COUNTRY

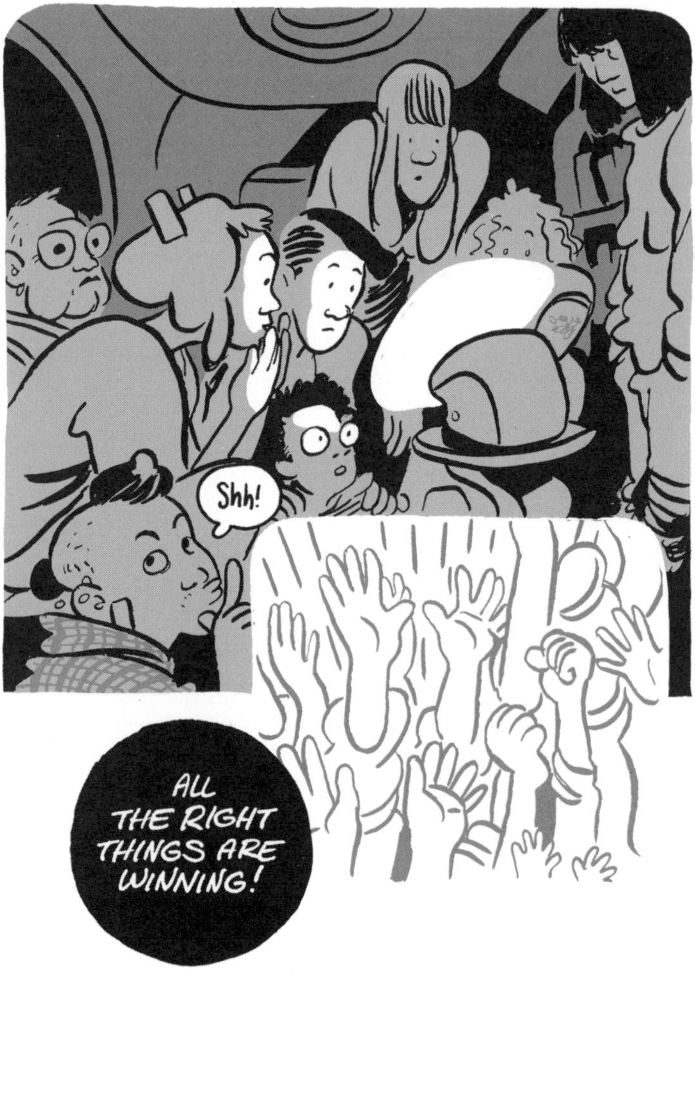
Shh!
ALL THE RIGHT THINGS ARE WINNING!

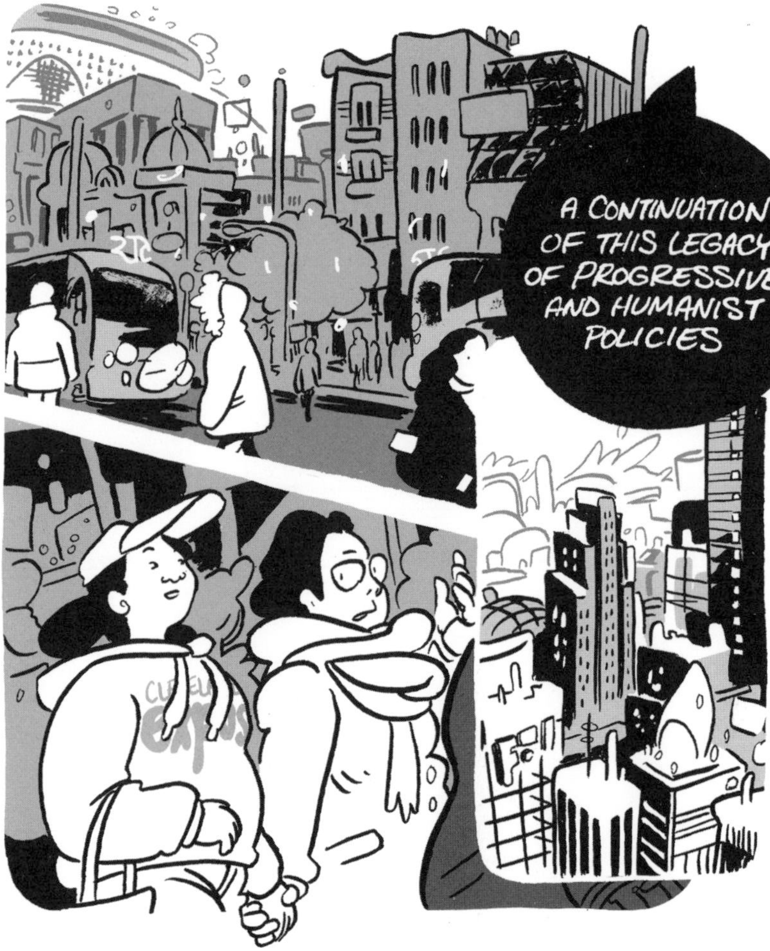
A CONTINUATION OF THIS LEGACY OF PROGRESSIVE AND HUMANIST POLICIES

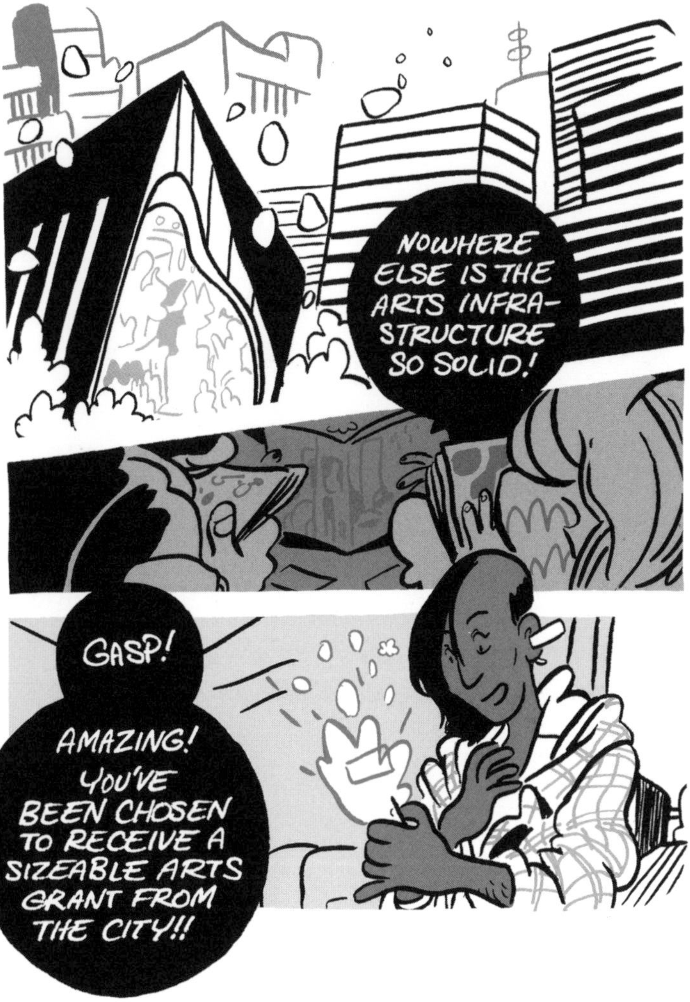
NOWHERE ELSE IS THE ARTS INFRA-STRUCTURE SO SOLID!
GASP!
AMAZING! YOU'VE BEEN CHOSEN TO RECEIVE A SIZEABLE ARTS GRANT FROM THE CITY!!

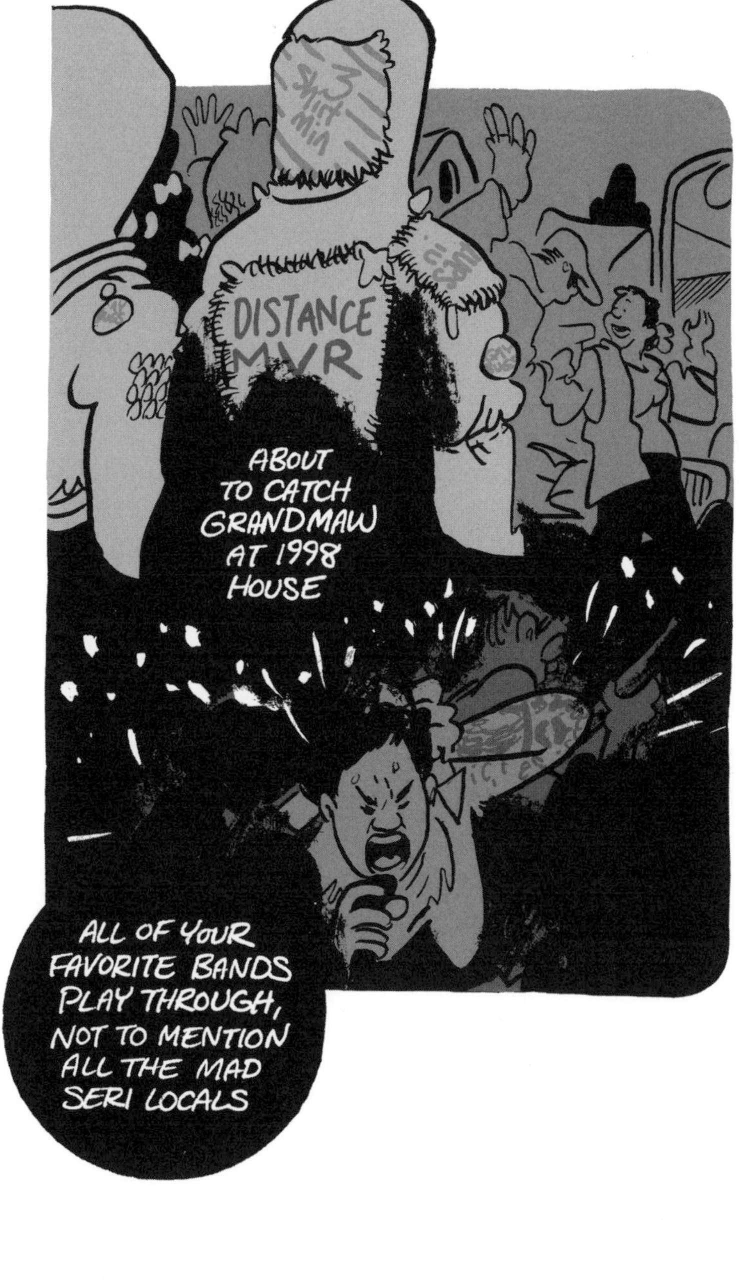
DISTANCE
MVR
ABOUT TO CATCH GRANDMAW AT 1998 HOUSE
ALL OF YOUR FAVORITE BANDS PLAY THROUGH, NOT TO MENTION ALL THE MAD SERI LOCALS

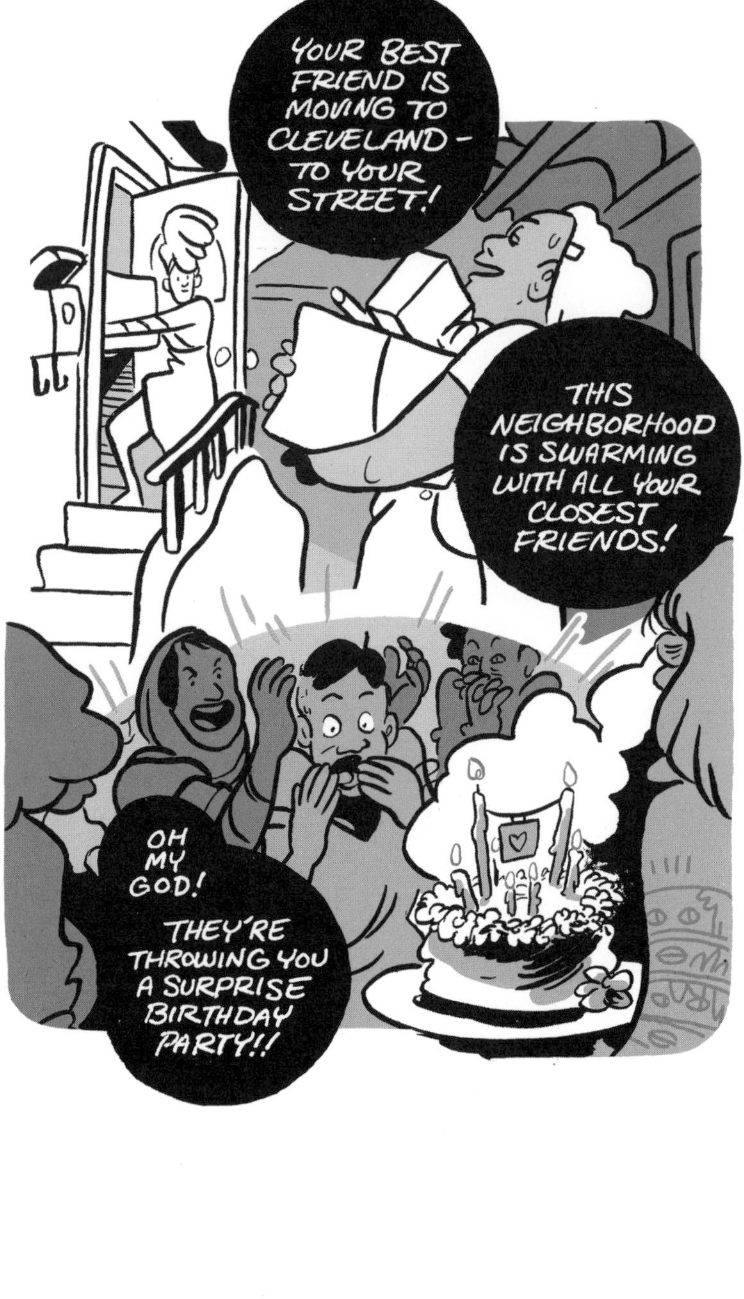
YOUR BEST FRIEND IS MOVING TO CLEVELAND - TO YOUR STREET!
THIS NEIGHBORHOOD IS SWARMING WITH ALL YOUR CLOSEST FRIENDS!
OH MY GOD!
THEY'RE THROWING YOU A SURPRISE BIRTHDAY PARTY!!

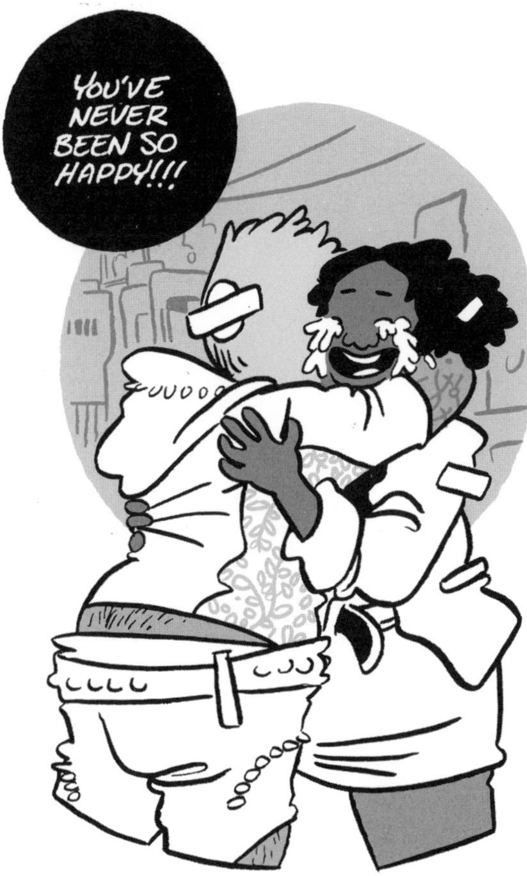
YOU'VE NEVER BEEN SO HAPPY!!!

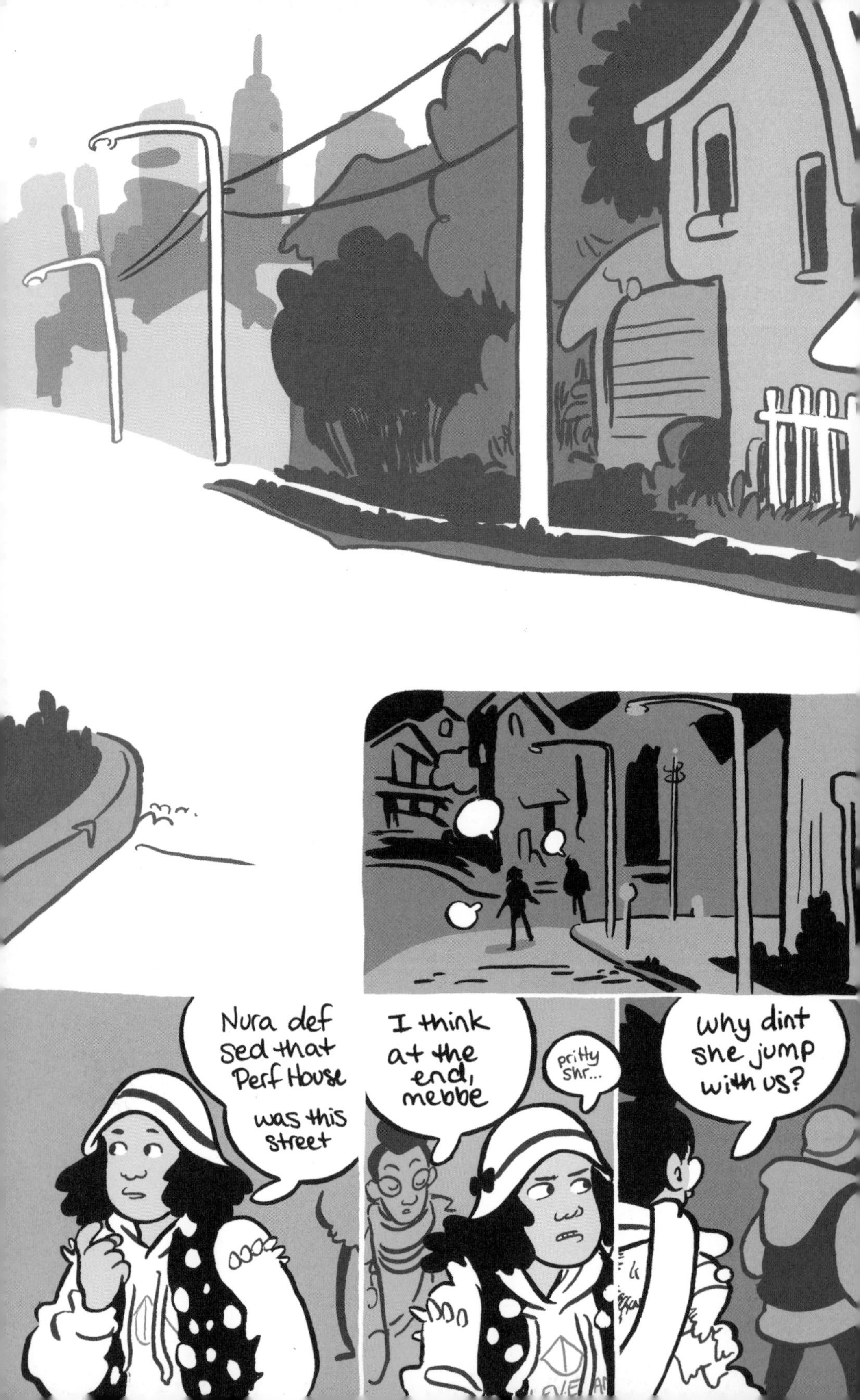
Nura def sed that Perf House was this street
I think at the end, mebbe
pritty shr...
why dint she jump with us?

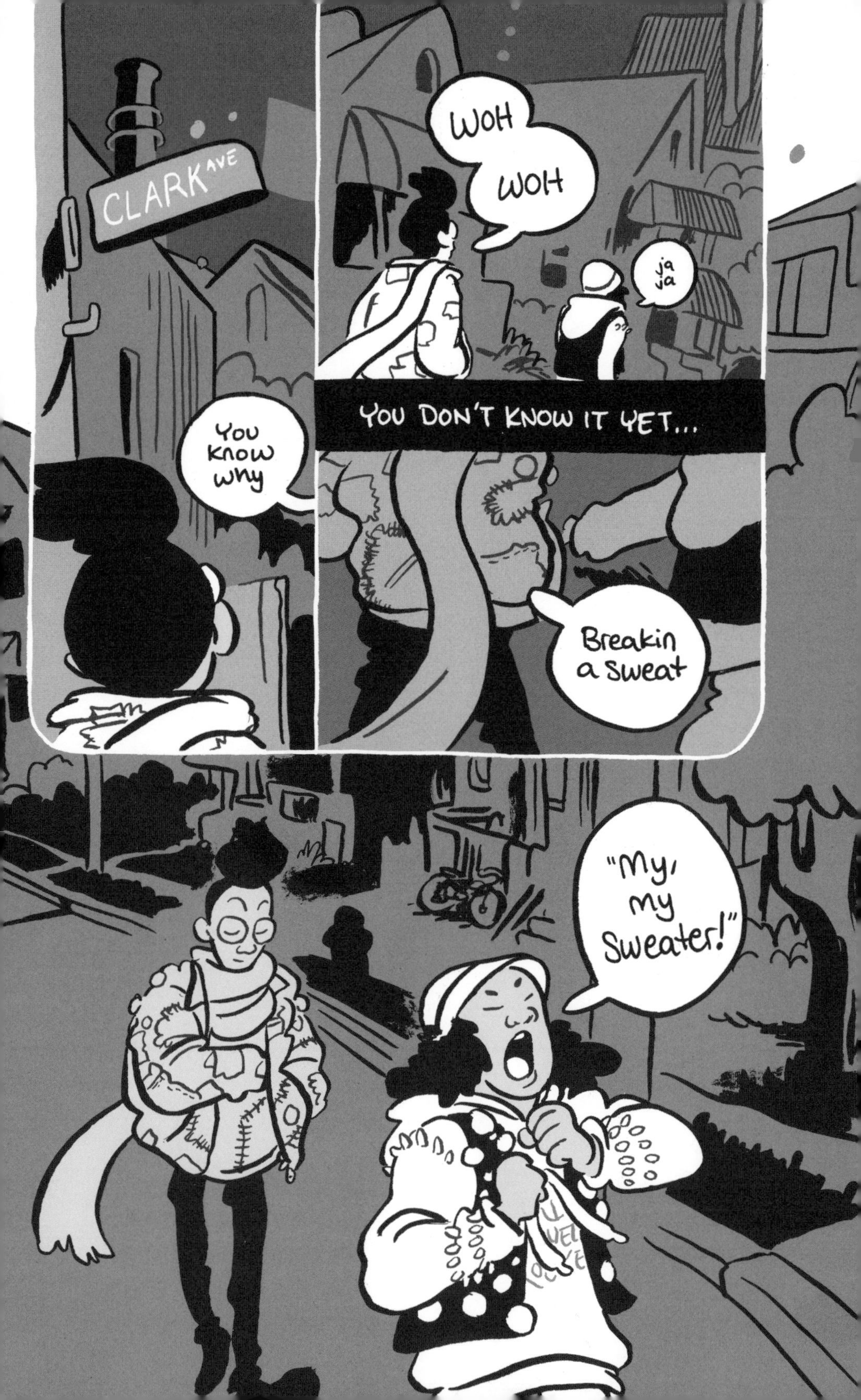
CLARK AVE
WOH
WOH
ja ja
YOU DON'T KNOW IT YET...
You know why
Breakin a sweat
"My, my Sweater!"

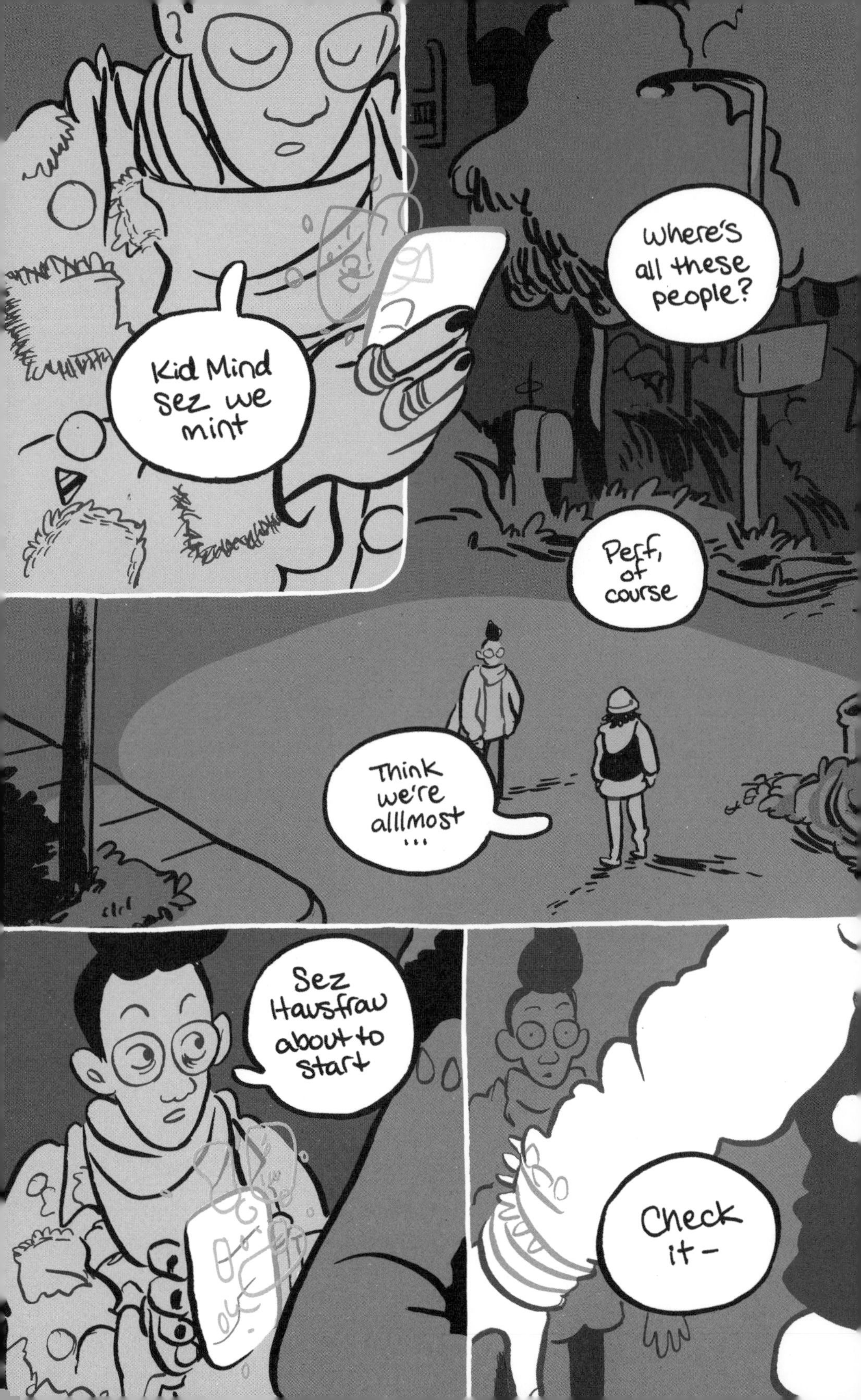
Kid Mind sez we mint
Where's all these people?
Peff, of course
Think we're alllmost ...
Sez Hausfrau about to start
Check it -

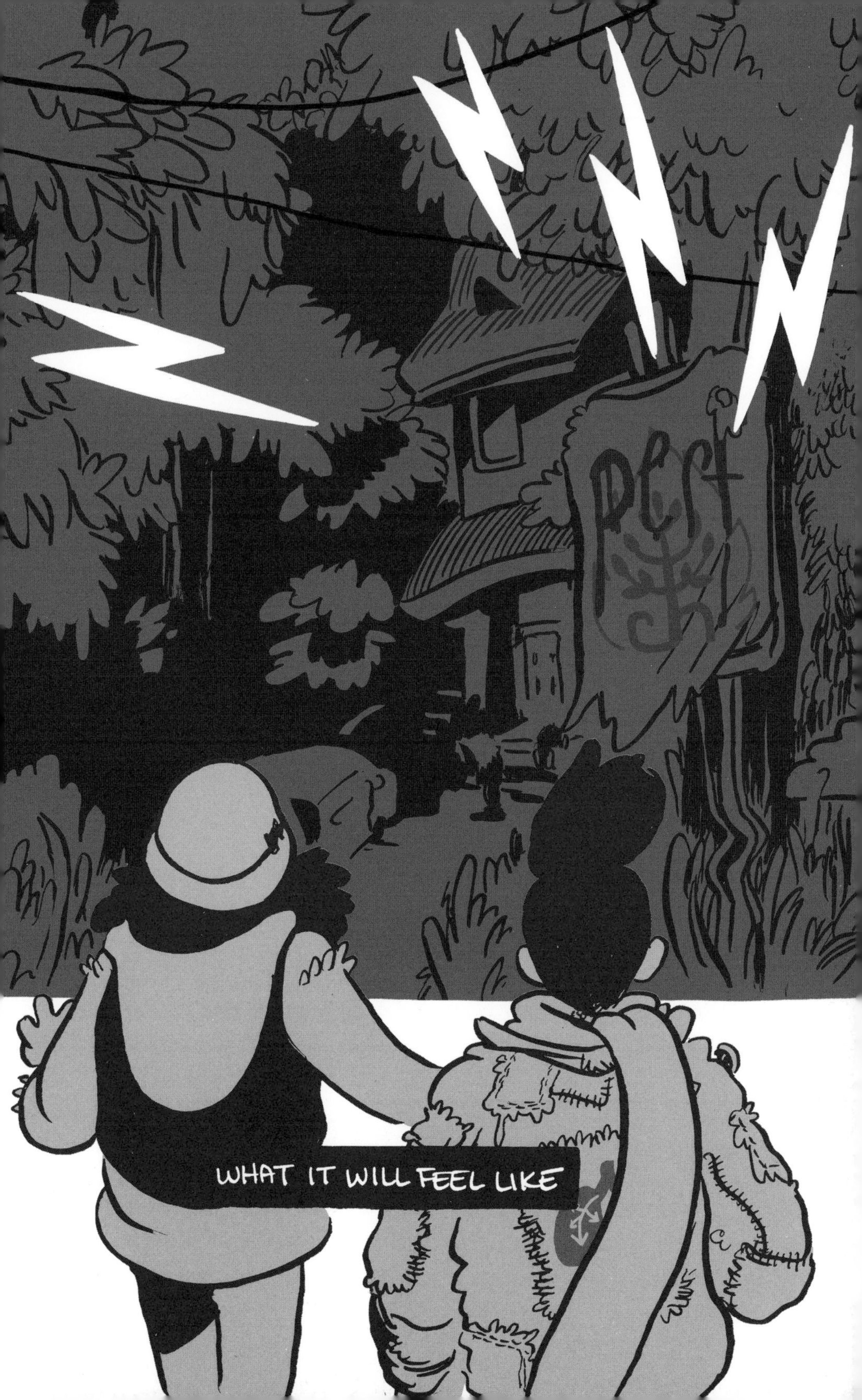
WHAT IT WILL FEEL LIKE

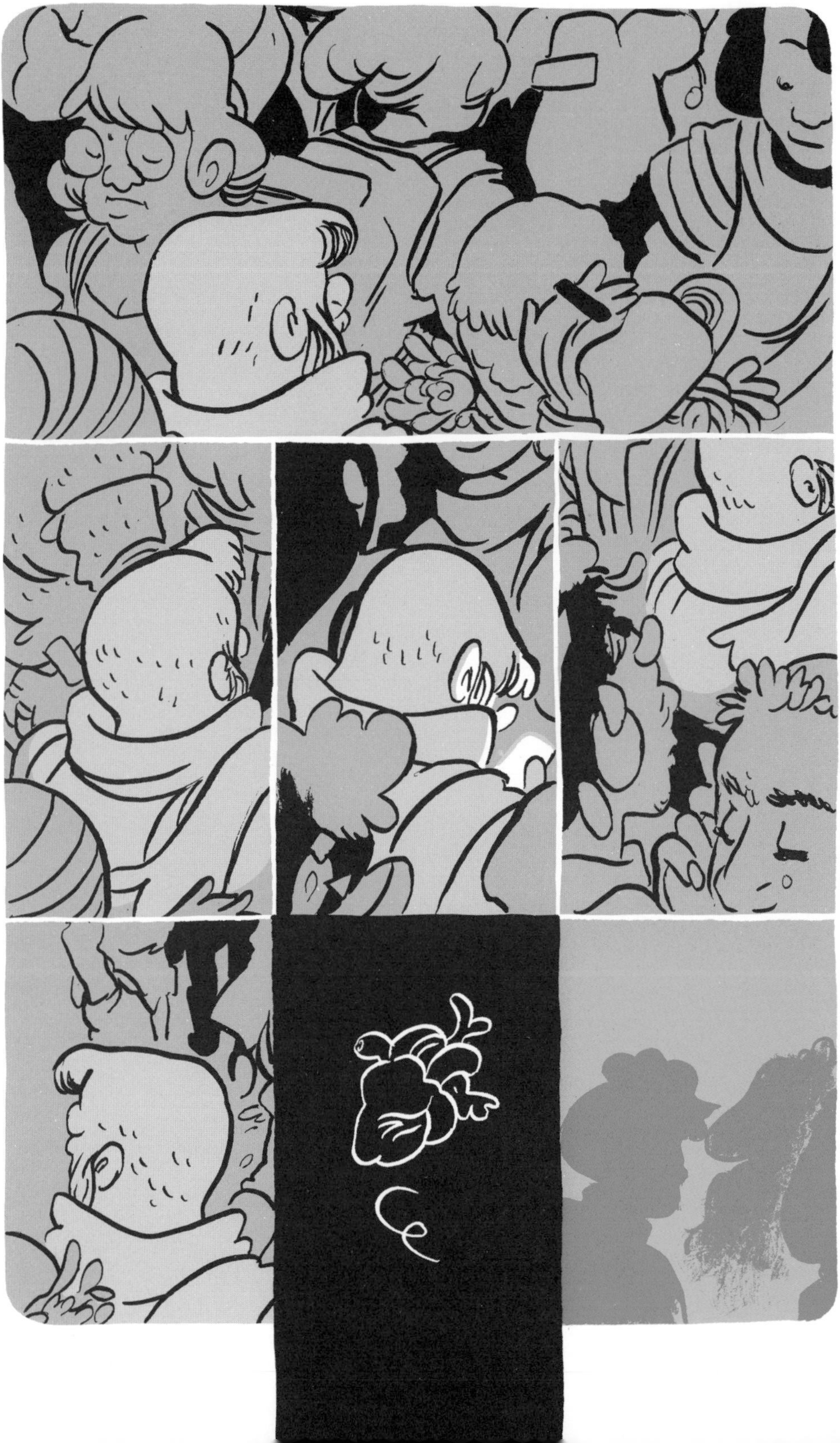

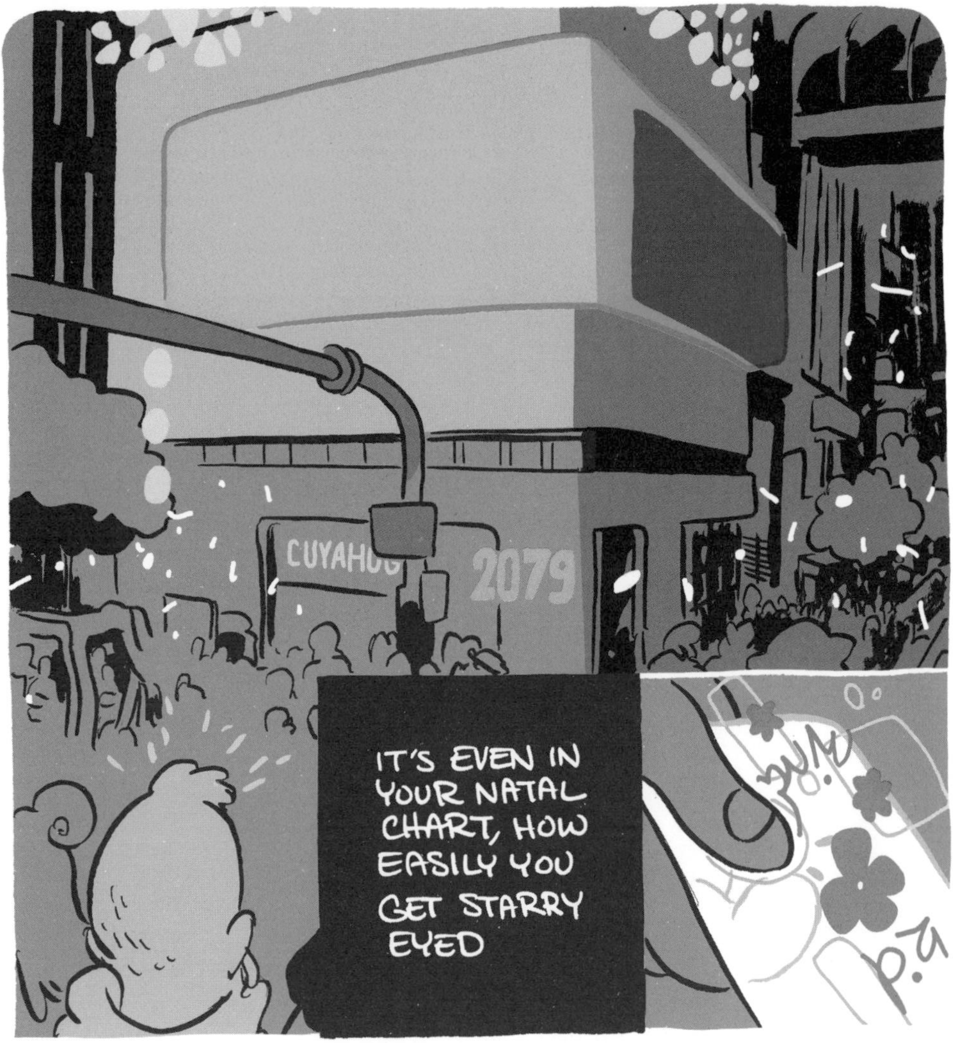
CUYAHOG
2079
IT'S EVEN IN YOUR NATAL CHART, HOW EASILY YOU GET STARRY EYED

THE KID MIND IS A GOVERNMENT SUBSIDIZED, CULTURAL THINKTANK THAT OTHERWISE OPERATES AUTONOMOUSLY

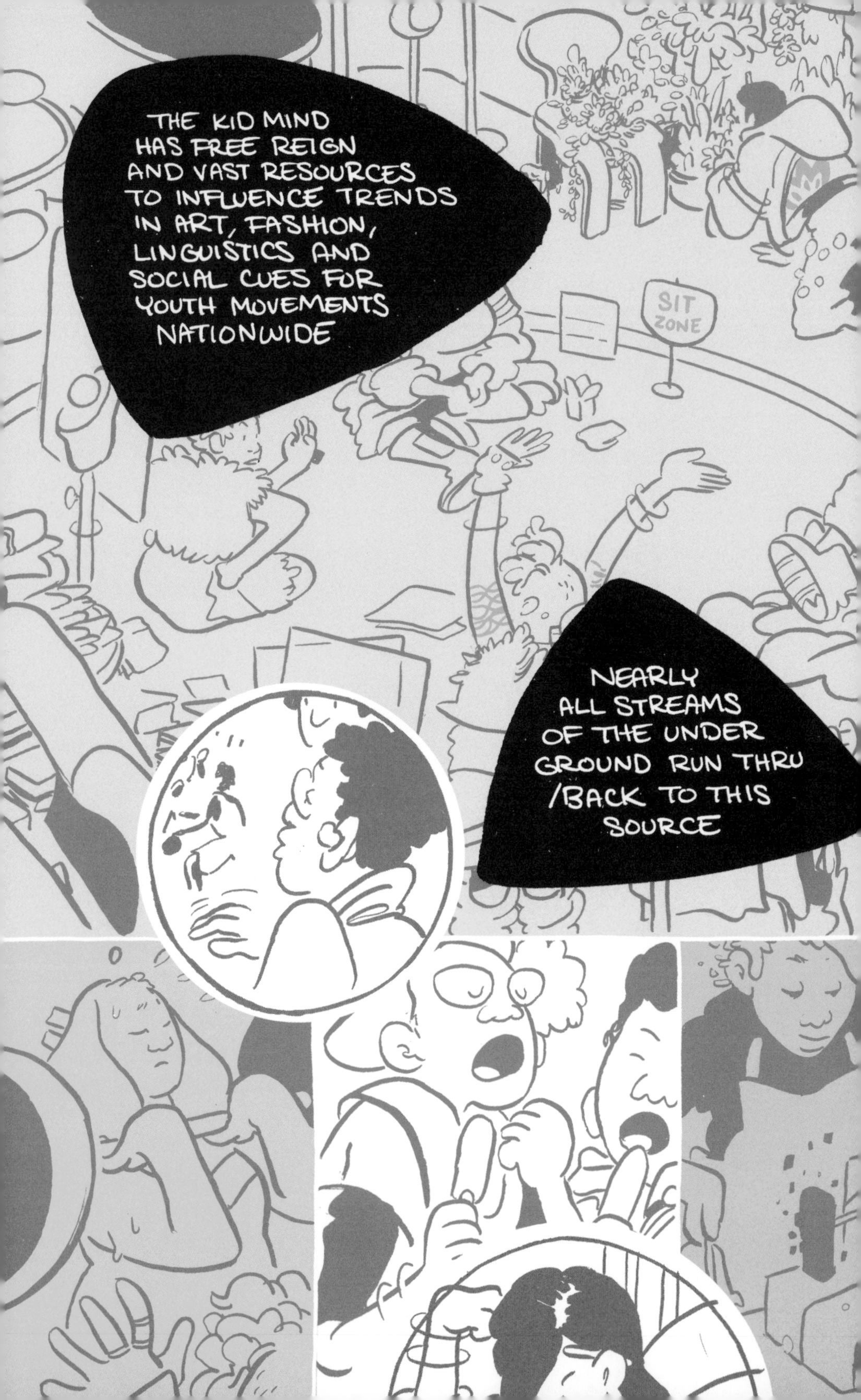
THE KID MIND HAS FREE REIGN AND VAST RESOURCES TO INFLUENCE TRENDS IN ART, FASHION, LINGUISTICS AND SOCIAL CUES FOR YOUTH MOVEMENTS NATIONWIDE
SIT ZONE
NEARLY ALL STREAMS OF THE UNDER GROUND RUN THRU /BACK TO THIS SOURCE

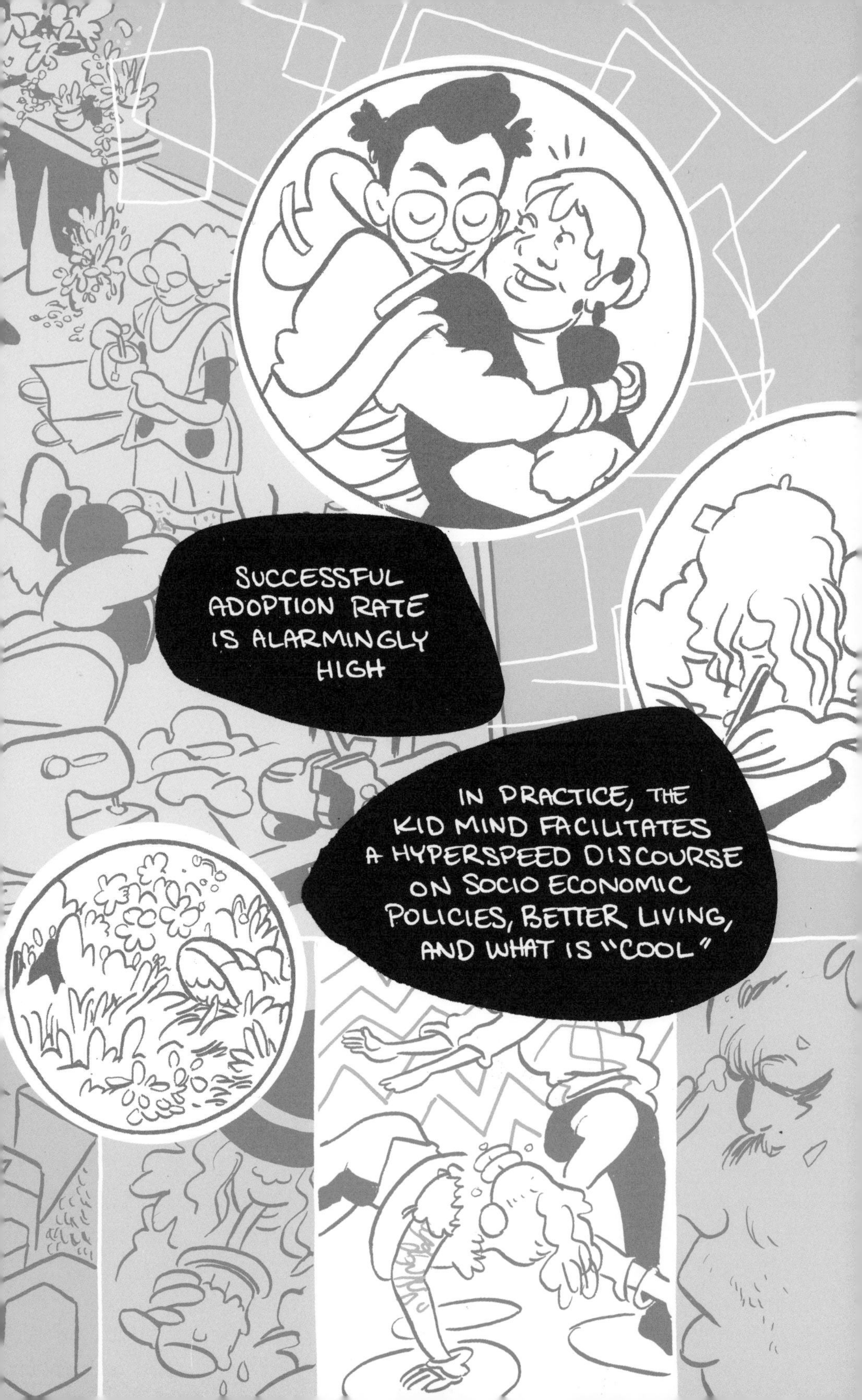
SUCCESSFUL ADOPTION RATE IS ALARMINGLY HIGH
IN PRACTICE, THE KID MIND FACILITATES A HYPERSPEED DISCOURSE ON SOCIO ECONOMIC POLICIES, BETTER LIVING, AND WHAT IS "COOL"

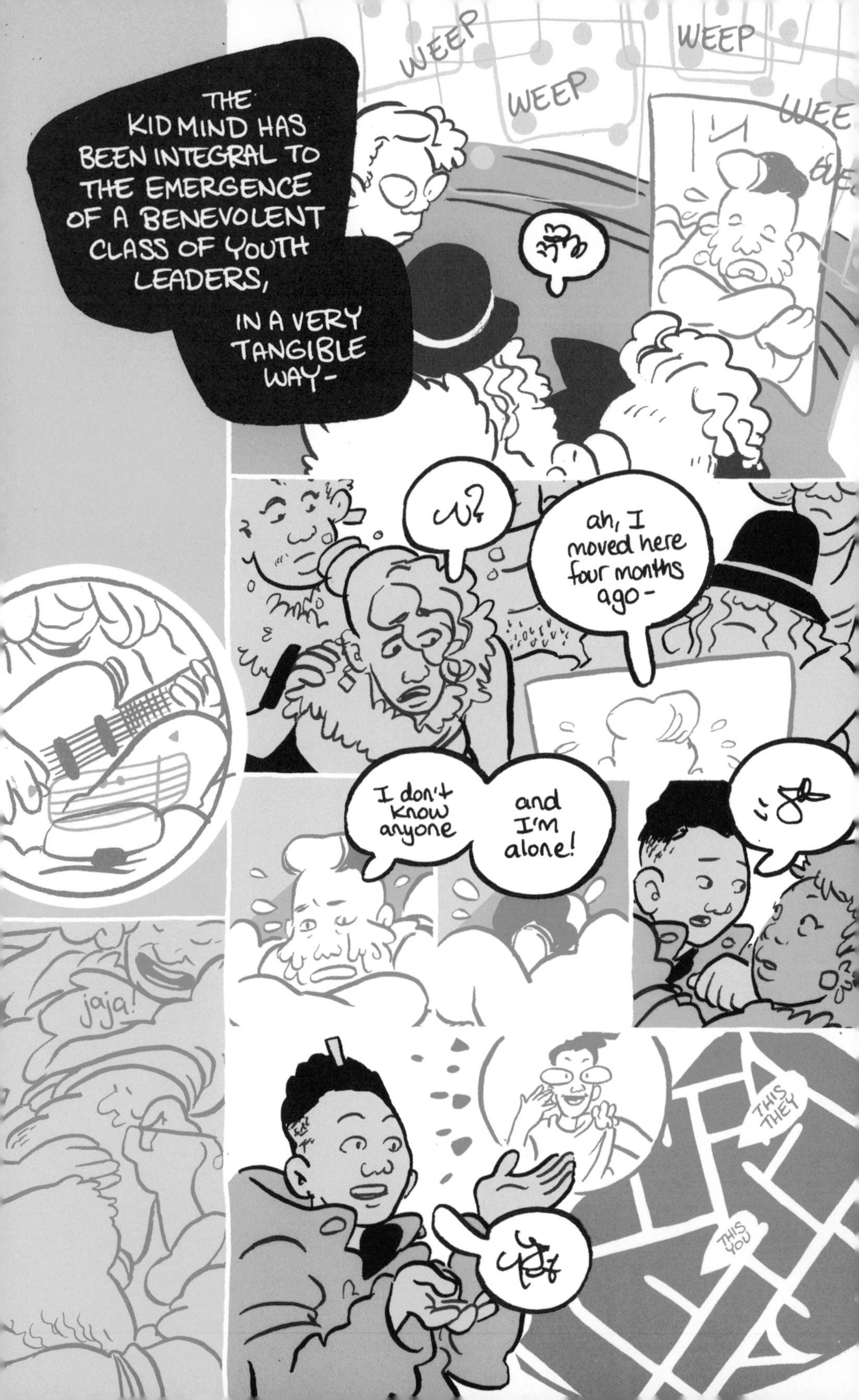

THE KID MIND HAS BEEN INTEGRAL TO THE EMERGENCE OF A BENEVOLENT CLASS OF YOUTH LEADERS,
IN A VERY TANGIBLE WAY-
WEEP
WEEP
WEEP
WEE
ah, I moved here four months ago-
I don't know anyone
and I'M alone!
jaja!
THIS THEY
THIS YOU

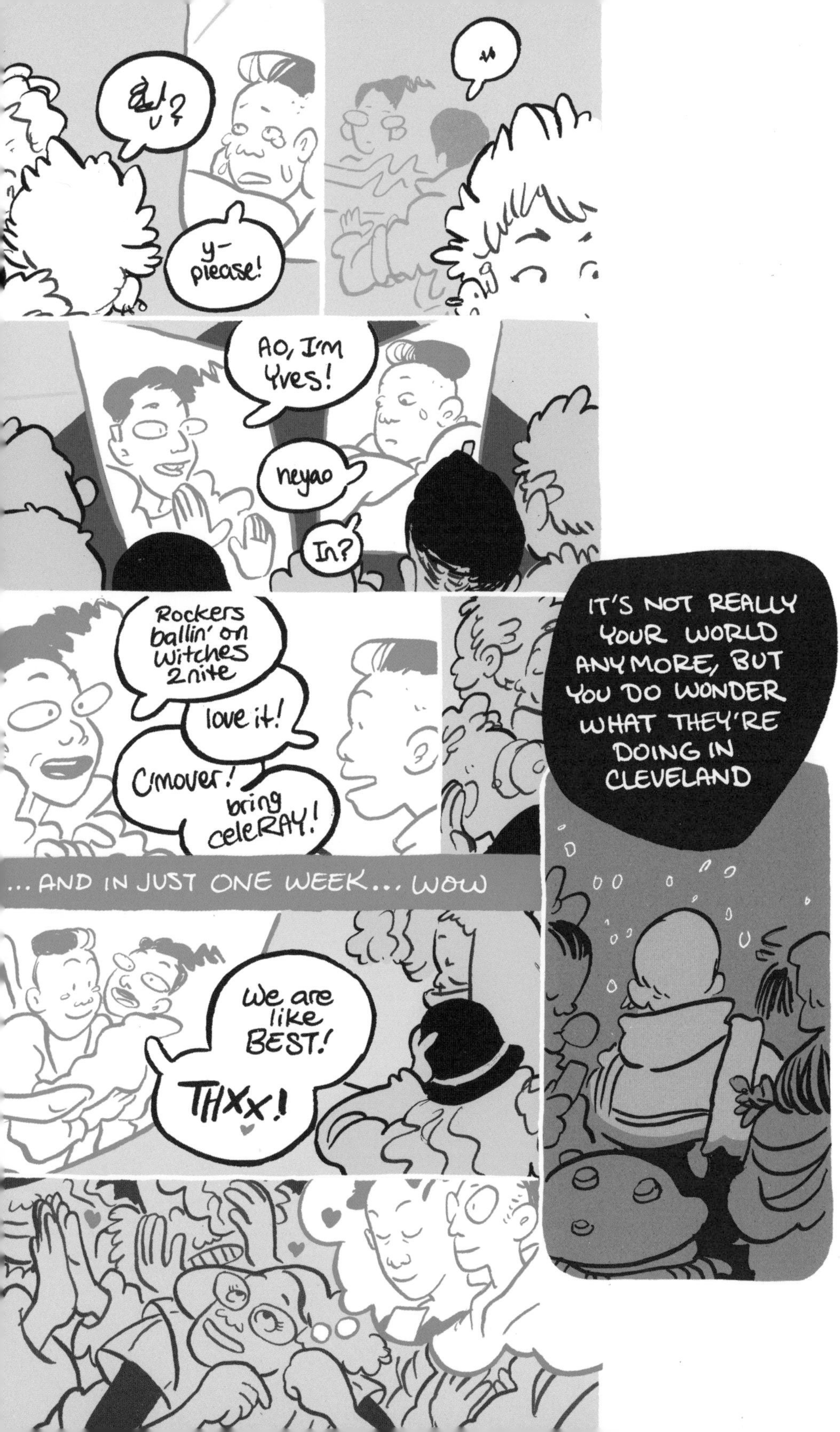

ร?
y-please!
AO, I'M Yves!
neyao
In?
Rockers ballin' on witches 2nite
love it!
C'mover!
bring celeRAY!
IT'S NOT REALLY YOUR WORLD ANYMORE, BUT YOU DO WONDER WHAT THEY'RE DOING IN CLEVELAND
... AND IN JUST ONE WEEK... WOW
We are like BEST!
THXx!

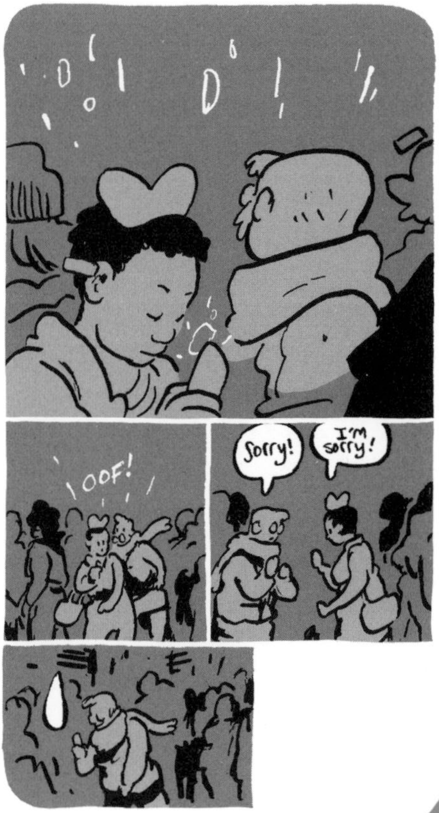
OOF!
Sorry!
I'm sorry!

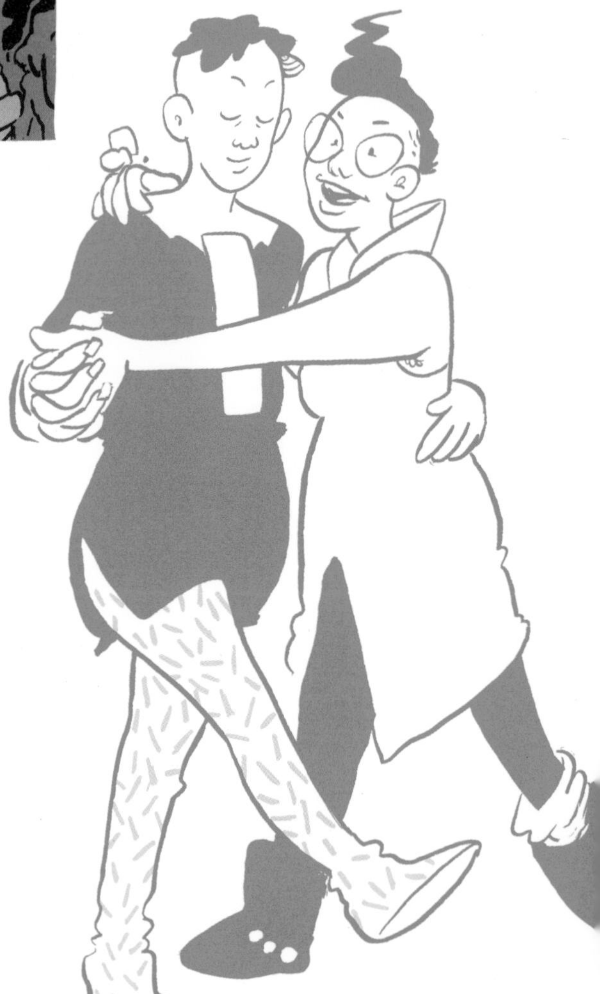

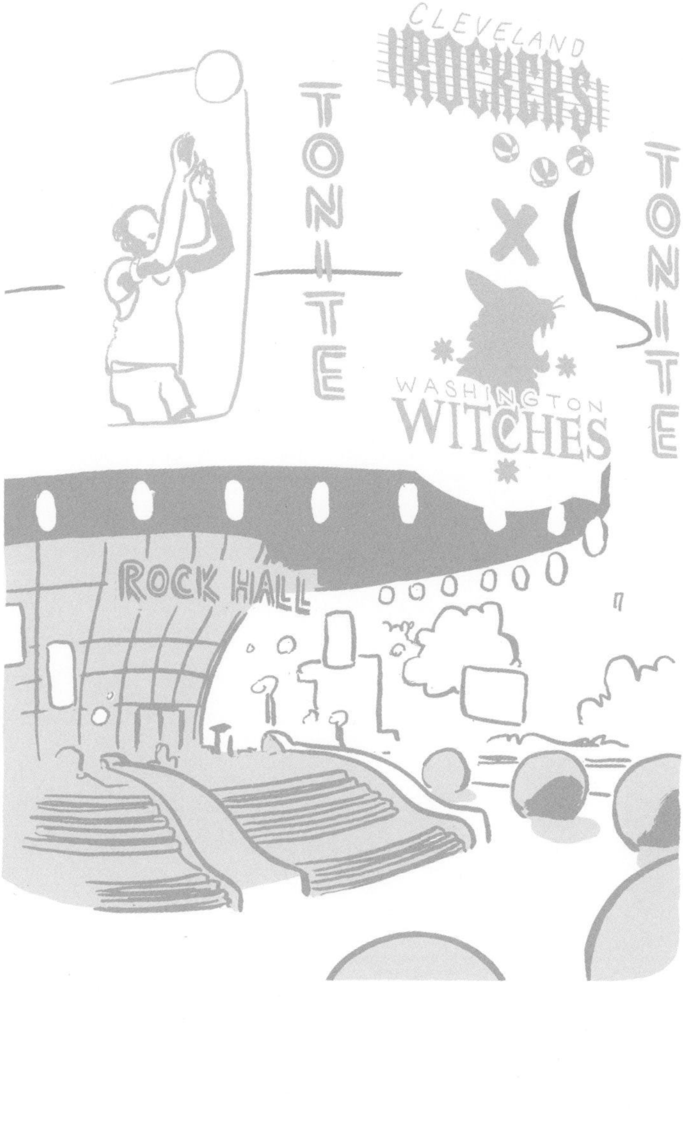

CLEVELAND
ROCKERS
TONITE
X
WASHINGTON
WITCHES
TONITE
ROCK HALL

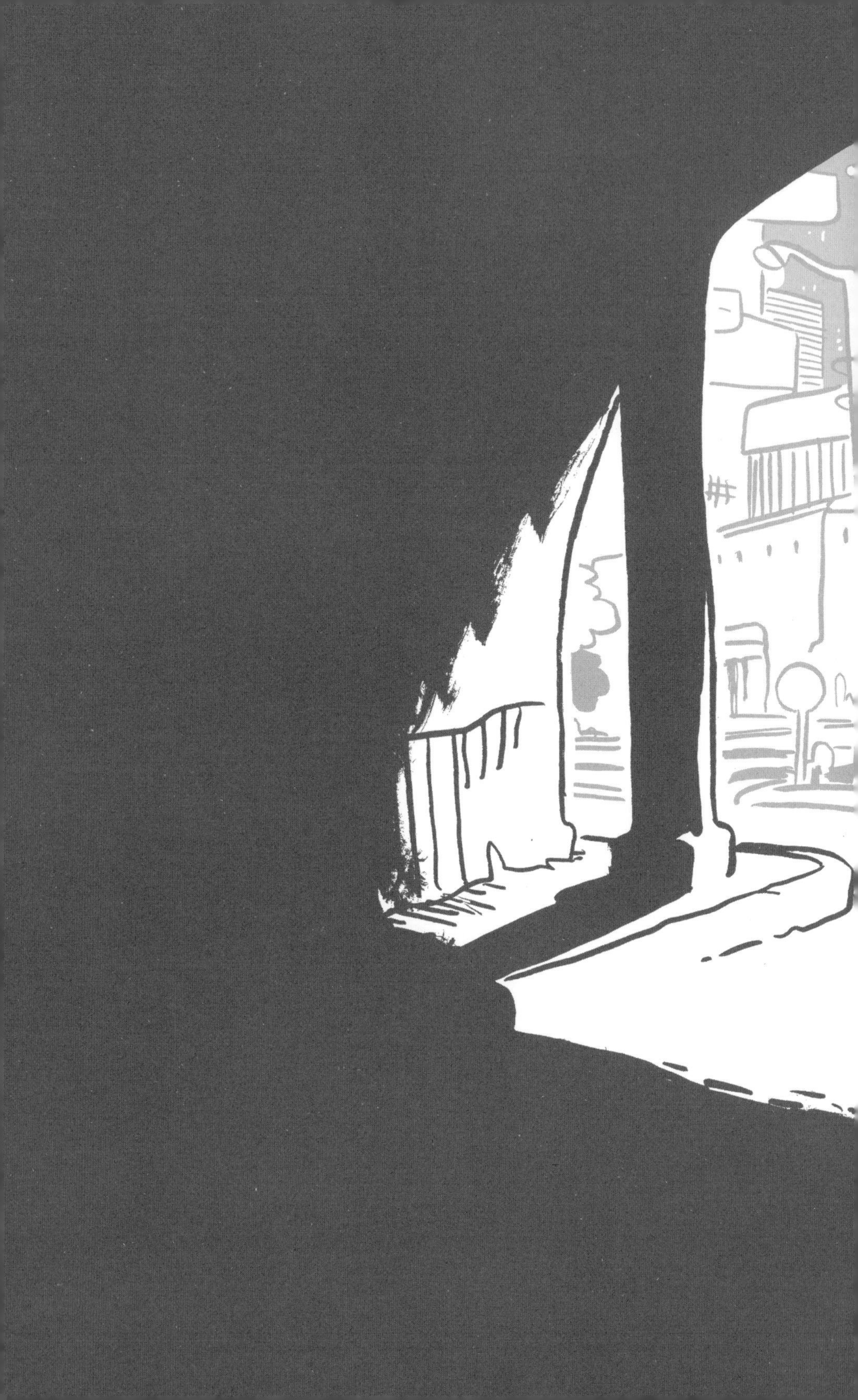

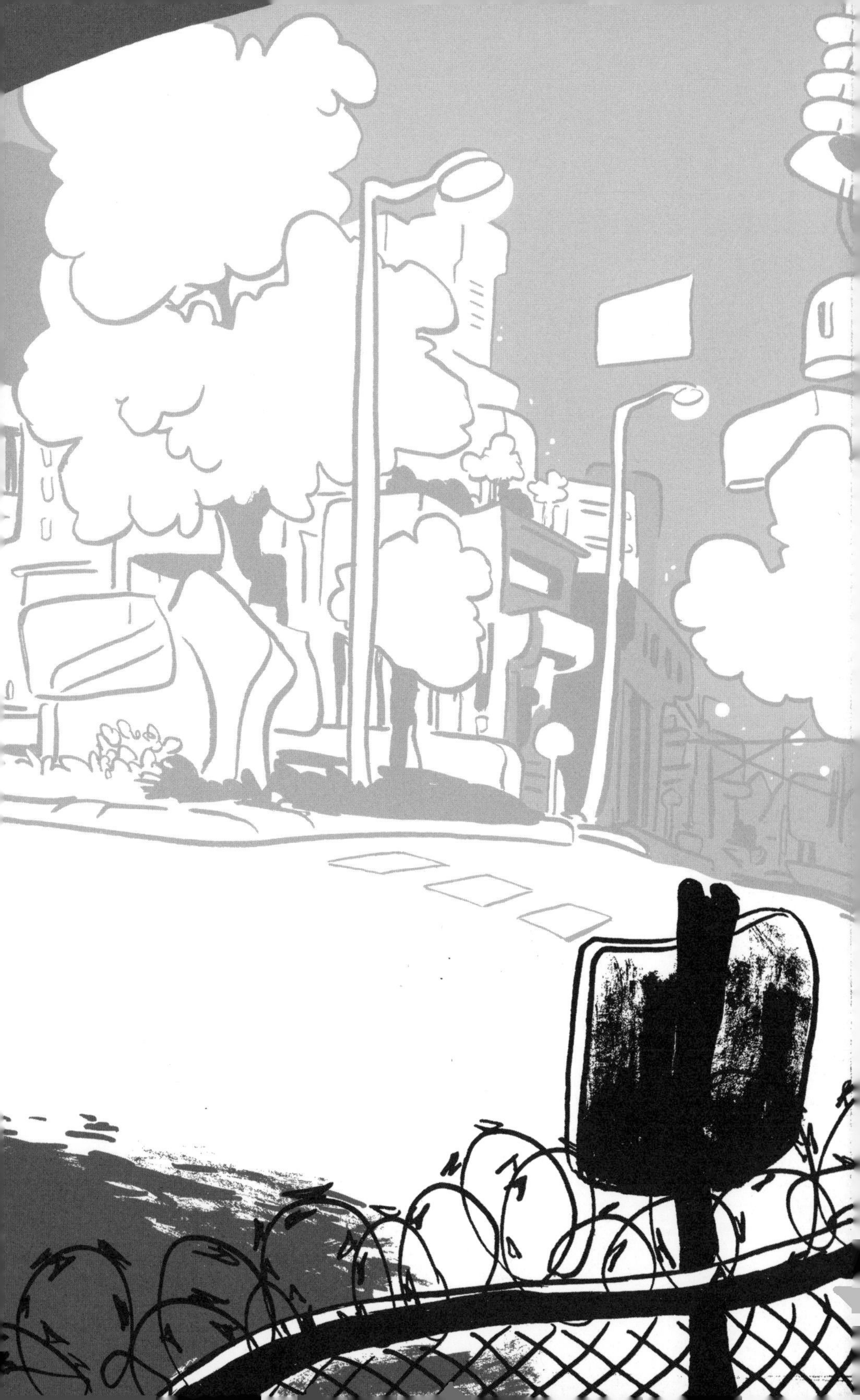

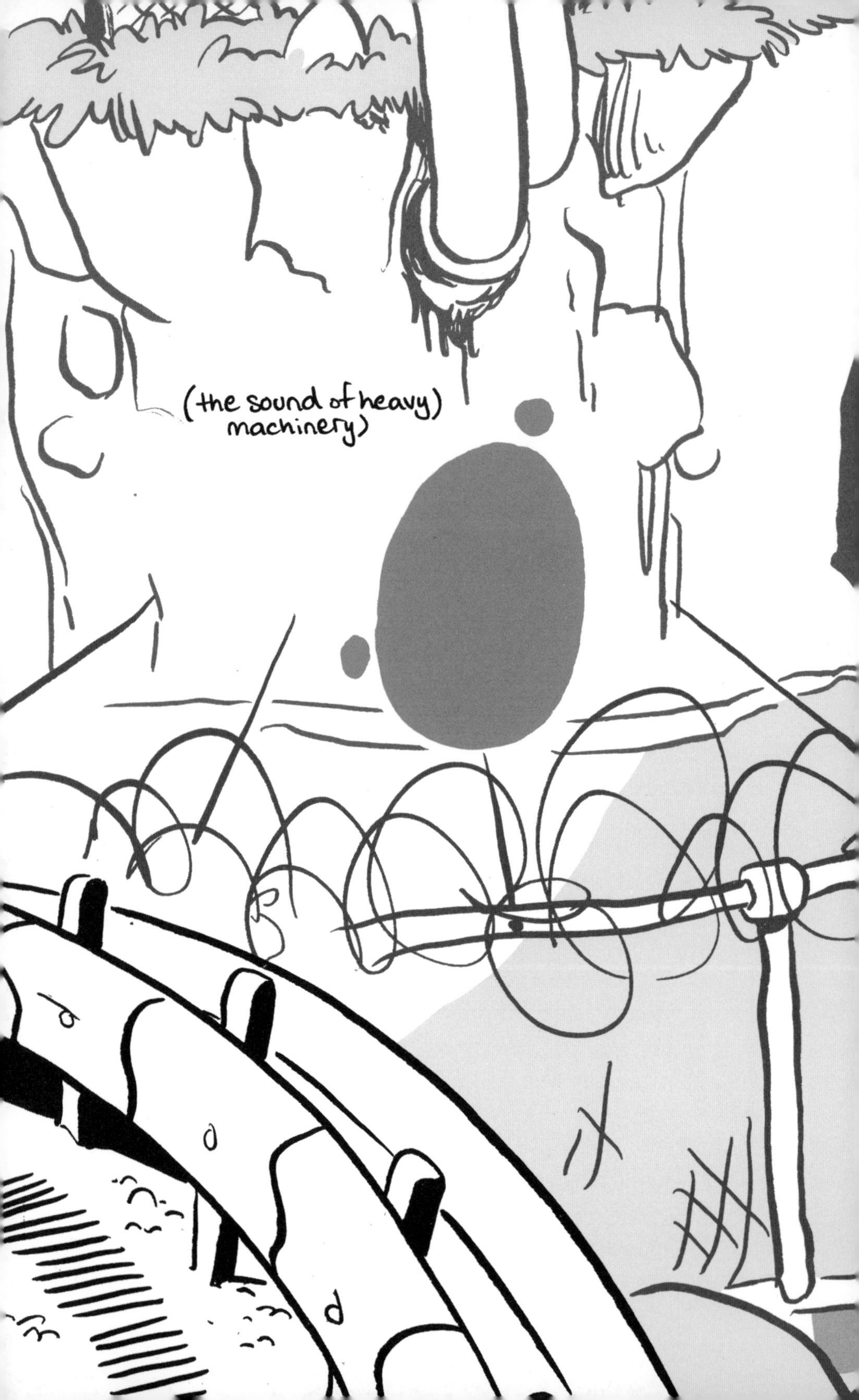
(the sound of heavy machinery)

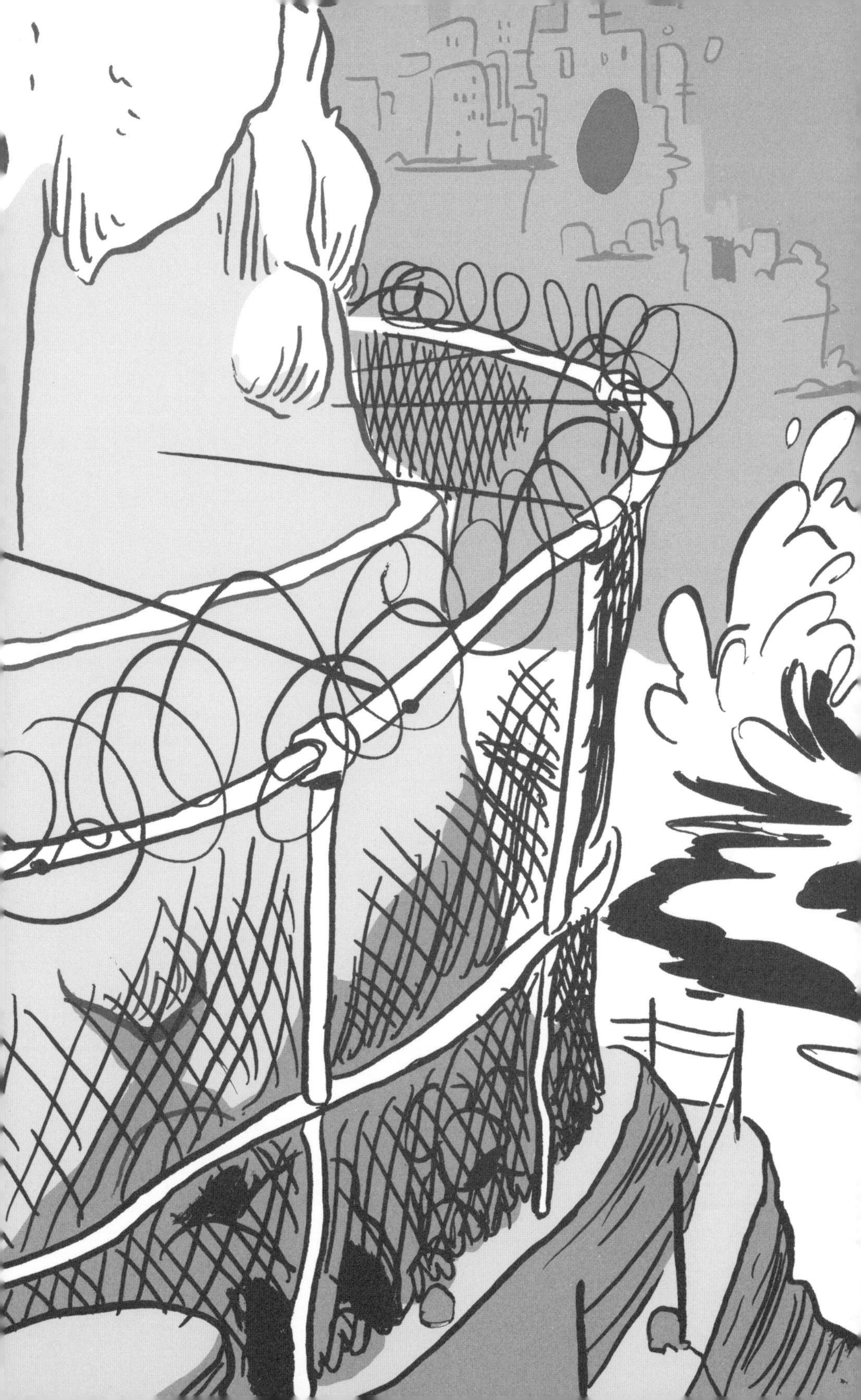

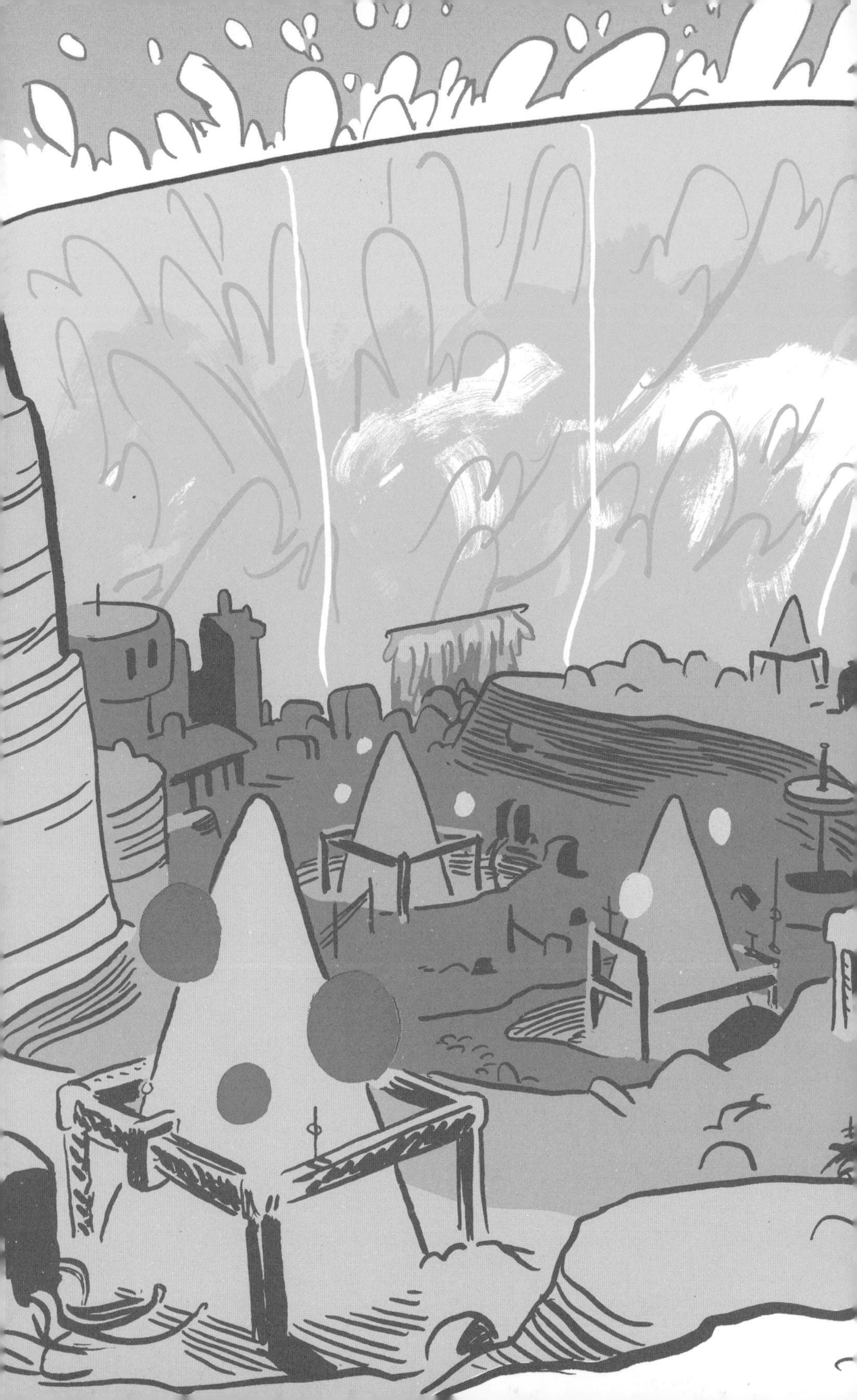

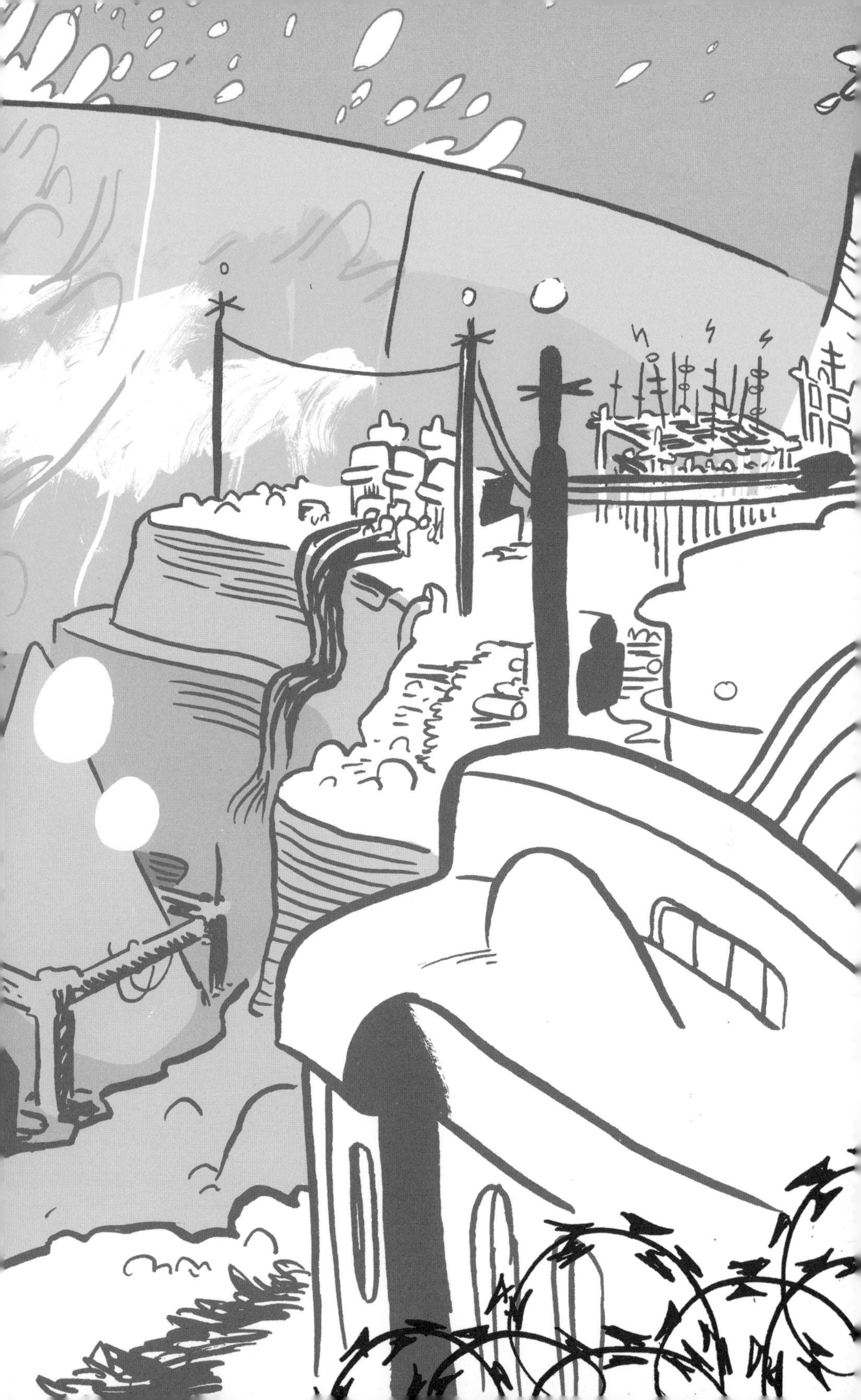

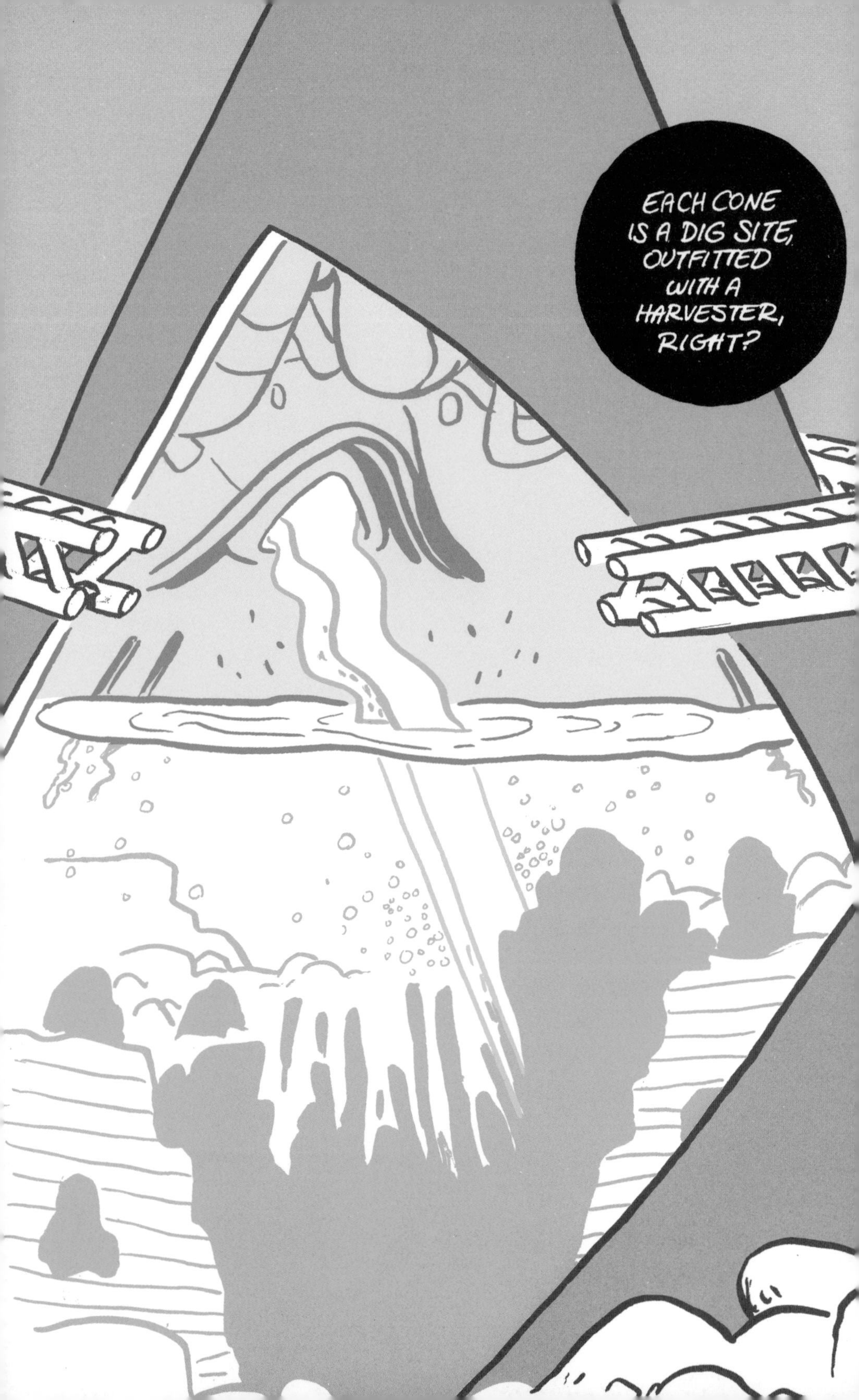
EACH CONE IS A DIG SITE, OUTFITTED WITH A HARVESTER, RIGHT?

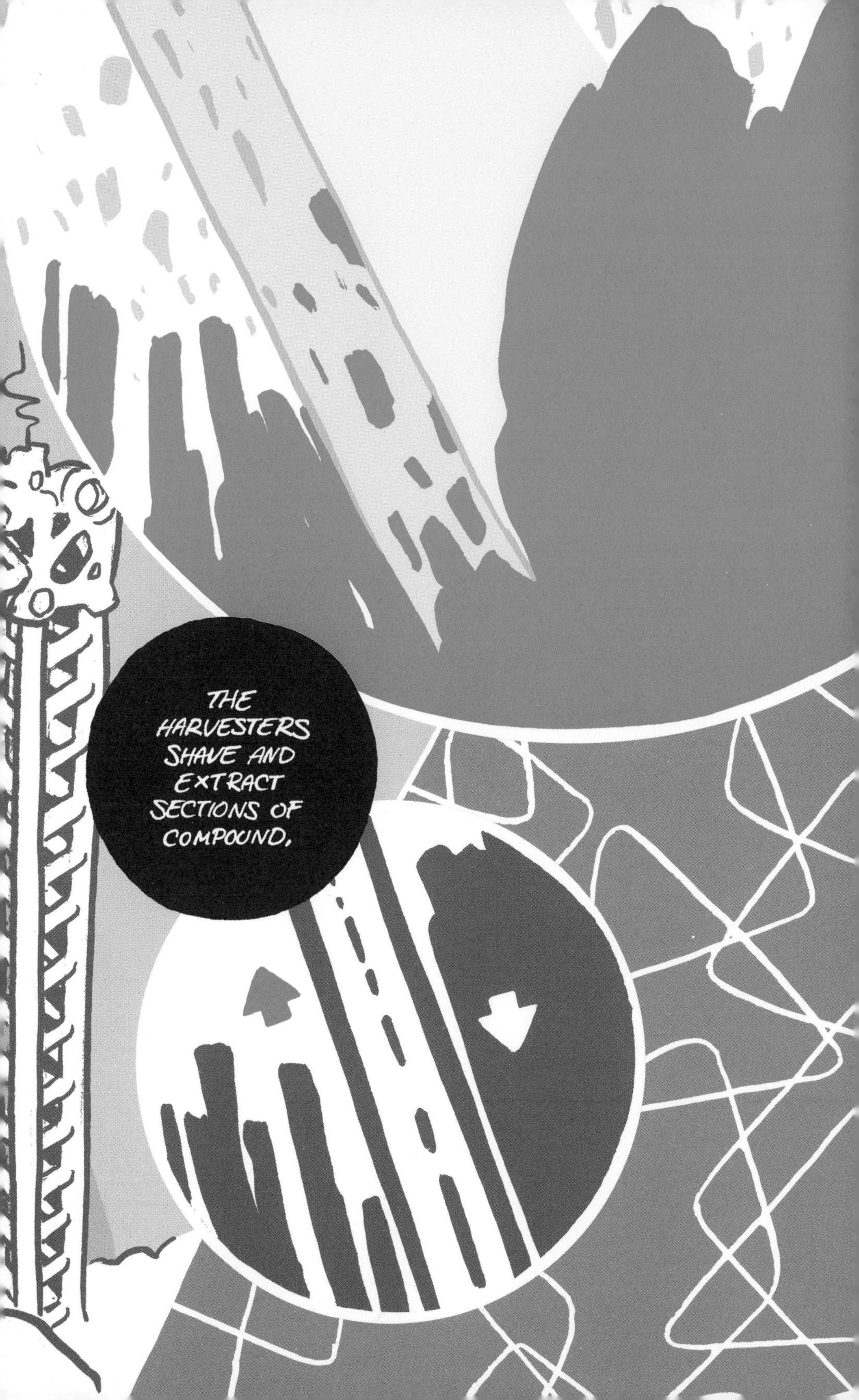
THE HARVESTERS SHAVE AND EXTRACT SECTIONS OF COMPOUND.

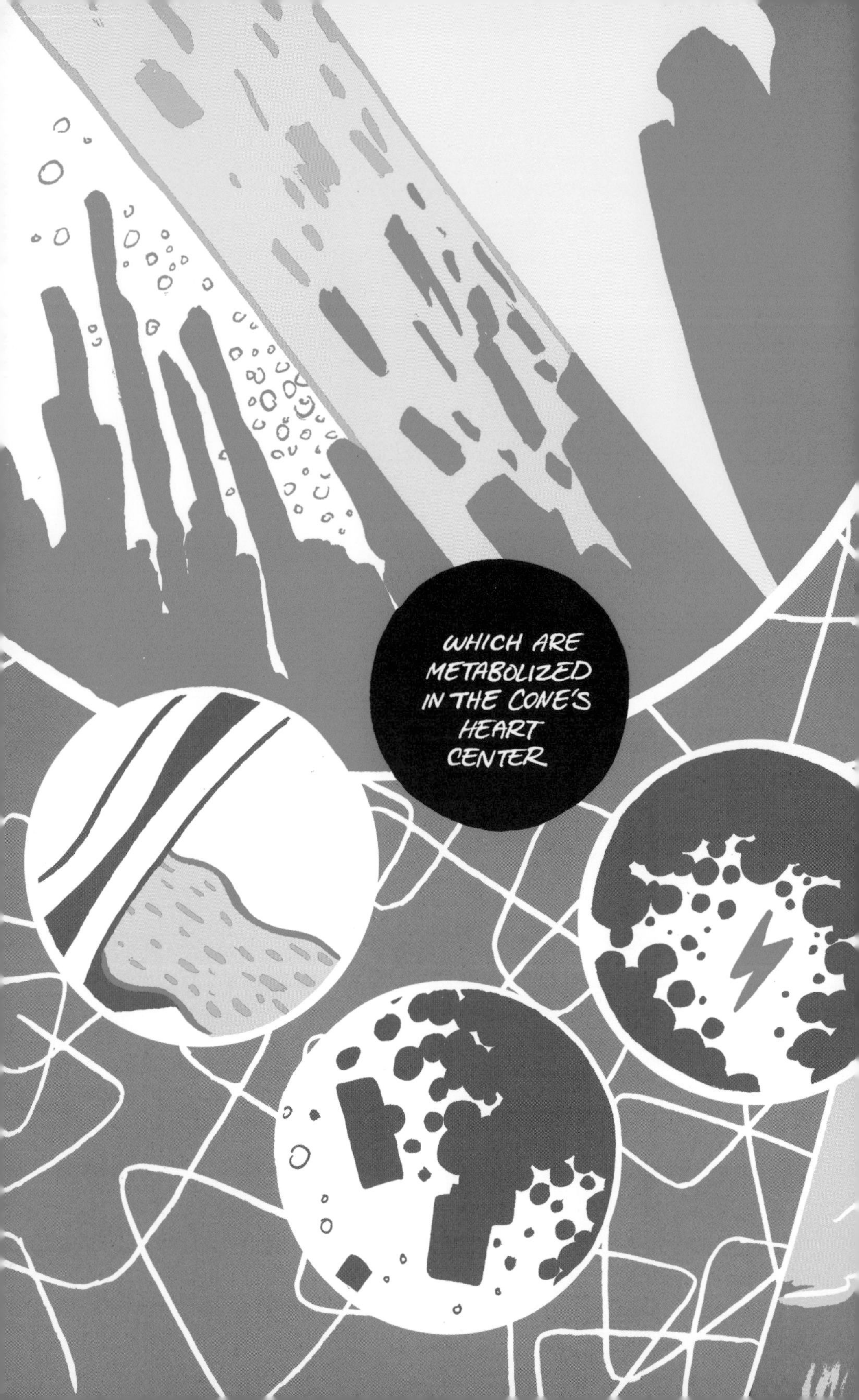
WHICH ARE METABOLIZED IN THE CONE'S HEART CENTER

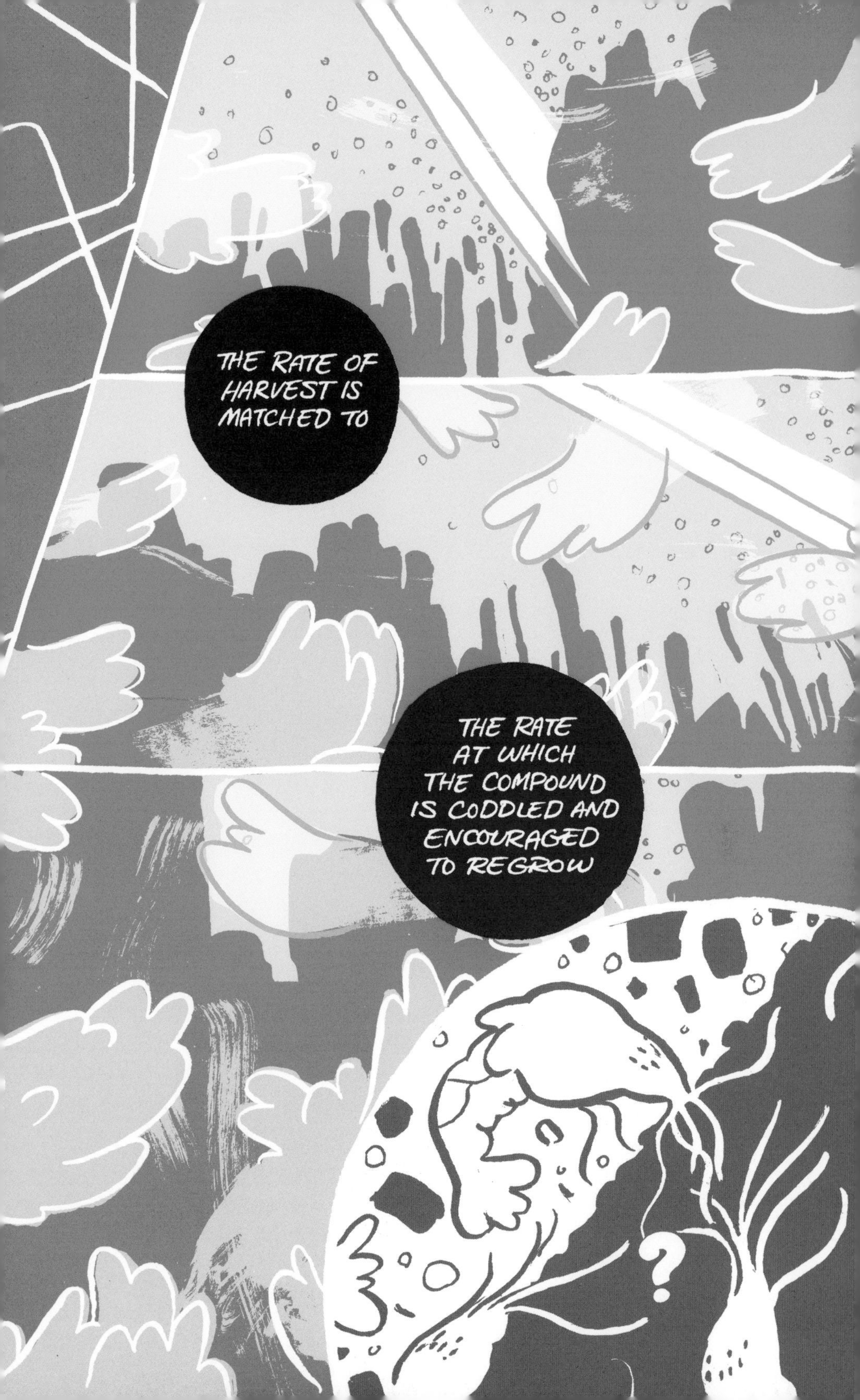
THE RATE OF HARVEST IS MATCHED TO
THE RATE AT WHICH THE COMPOUND IS CODDLED AND ENCOURAGED TO REGROW
?

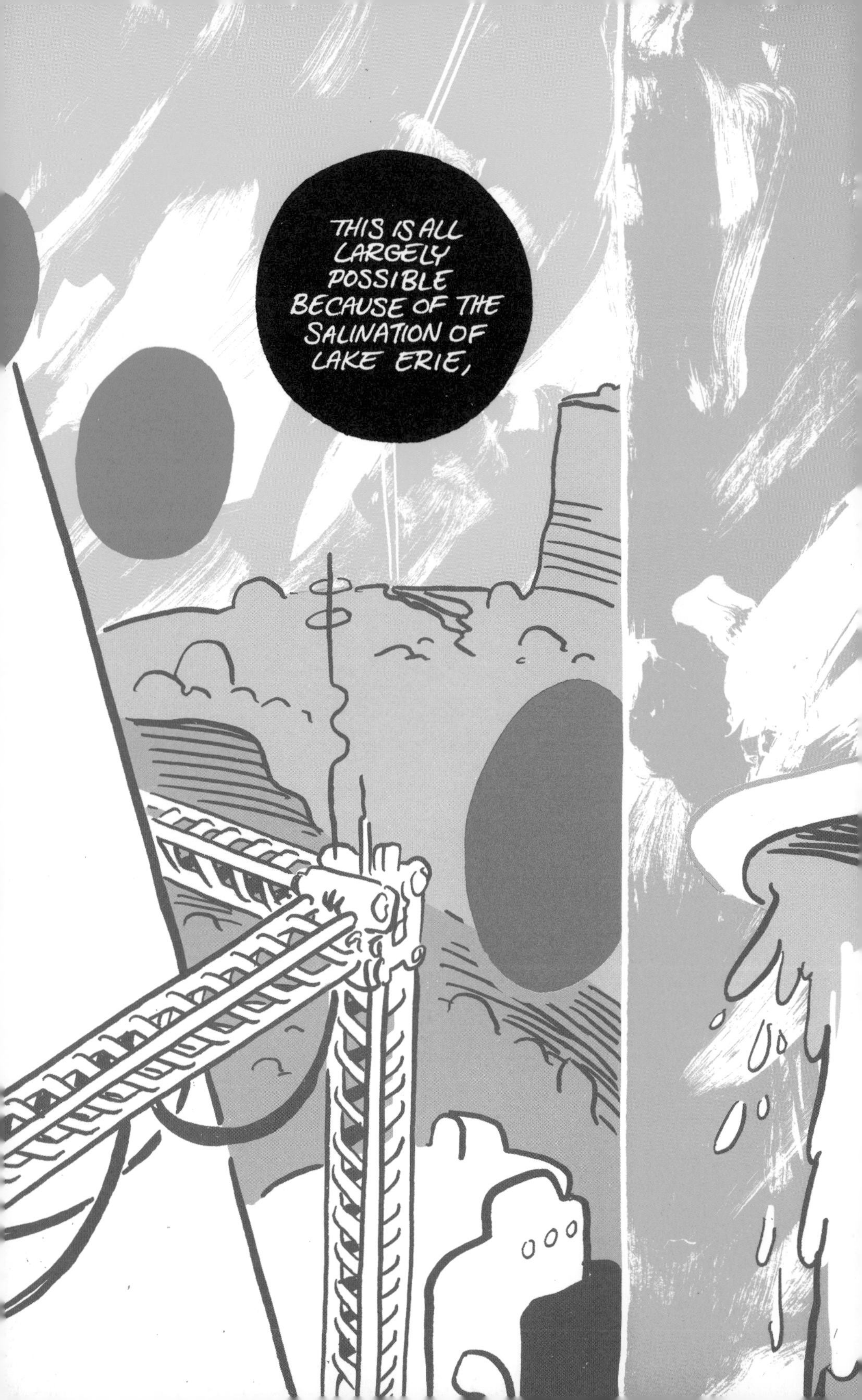
THIS IS ALL LARGELY POSSIBLE BECAUSE OF THE SALINATION OF LAKE ERIE,

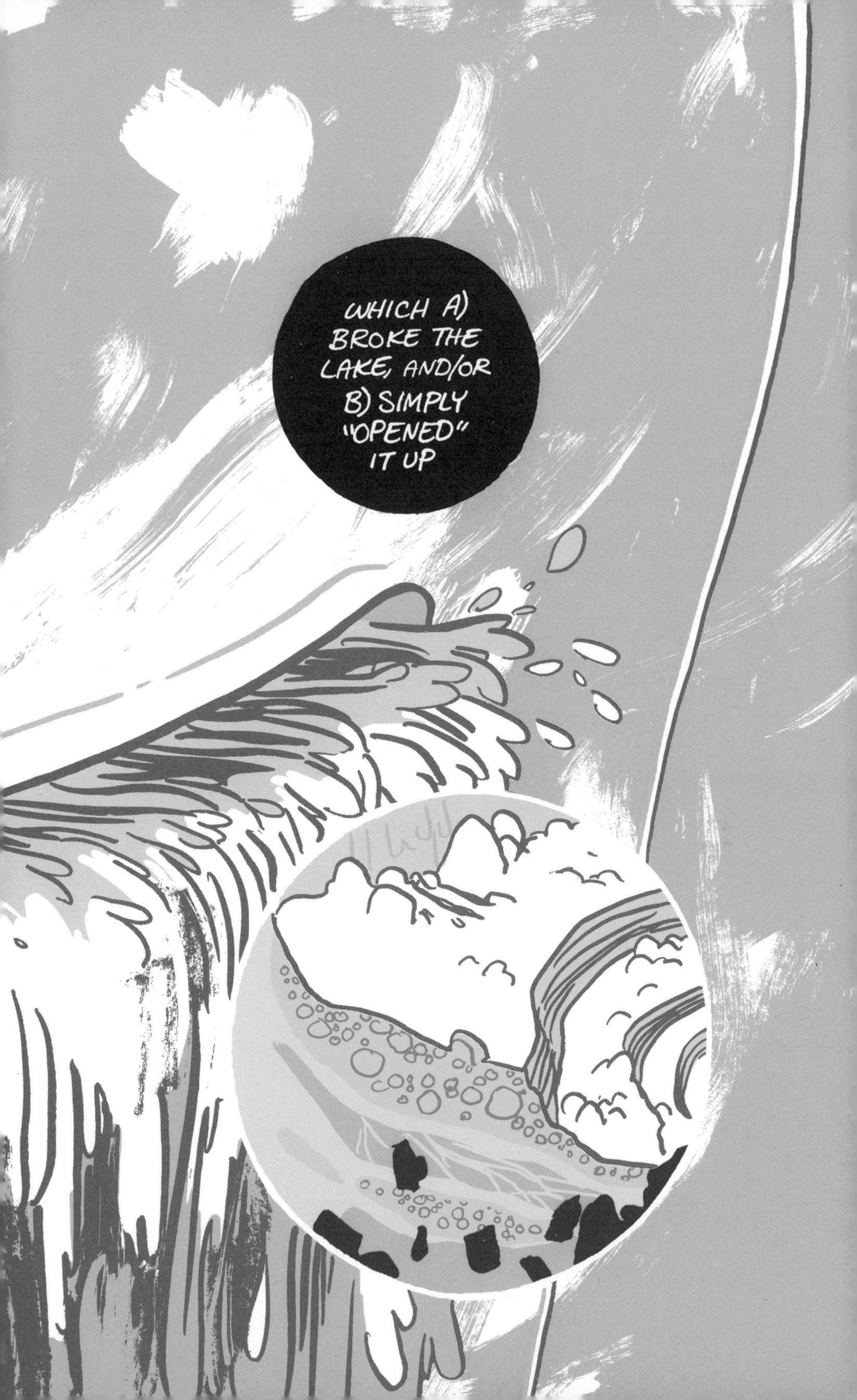
WHICH A) BROKE THE LAKE, AND/OR B) SIMPLY "OPENED" IT UP

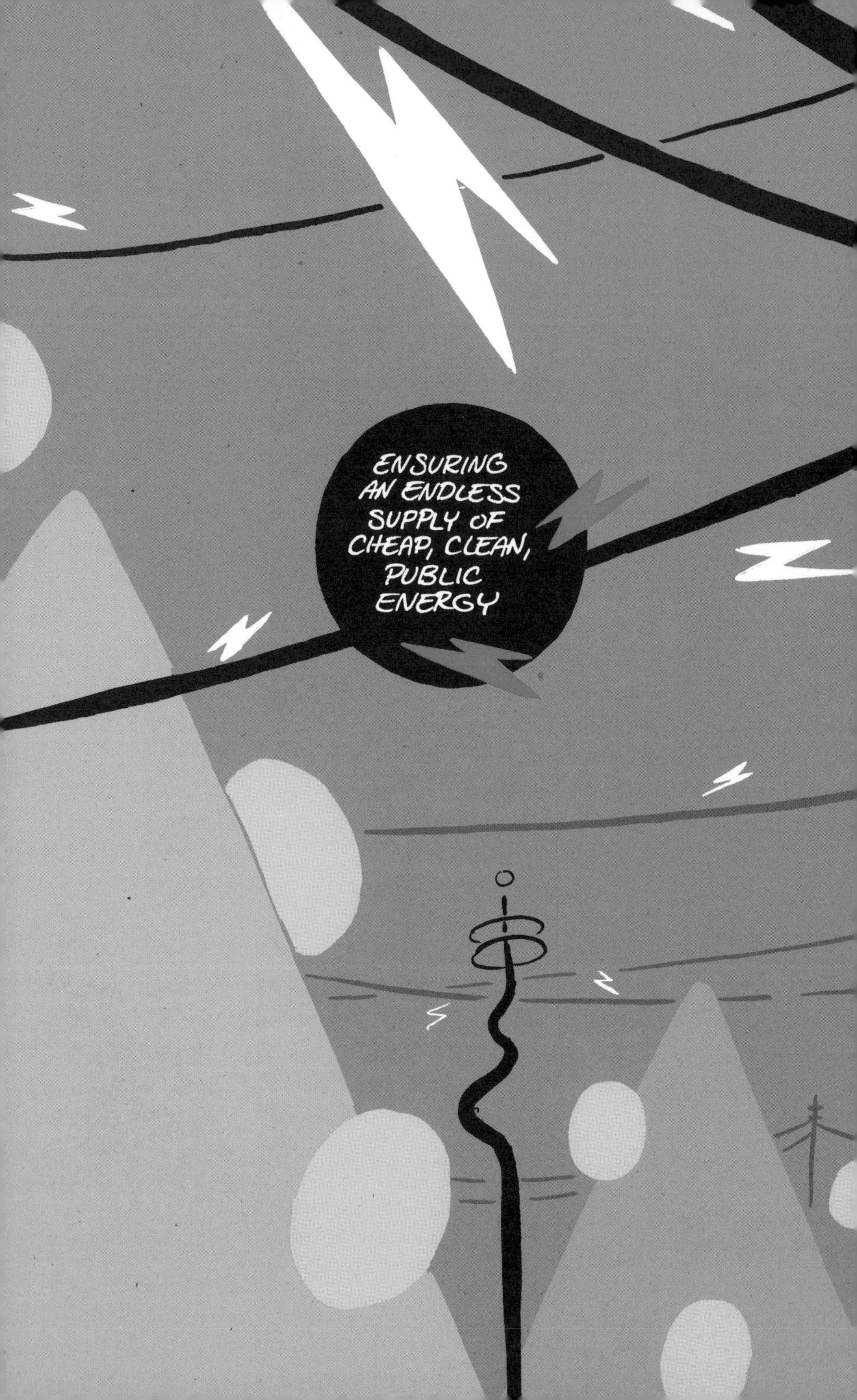
ENSURING AN ENDLESS SUPPLY OF CHEAP, CLEAN, PUBLIC ENERGY

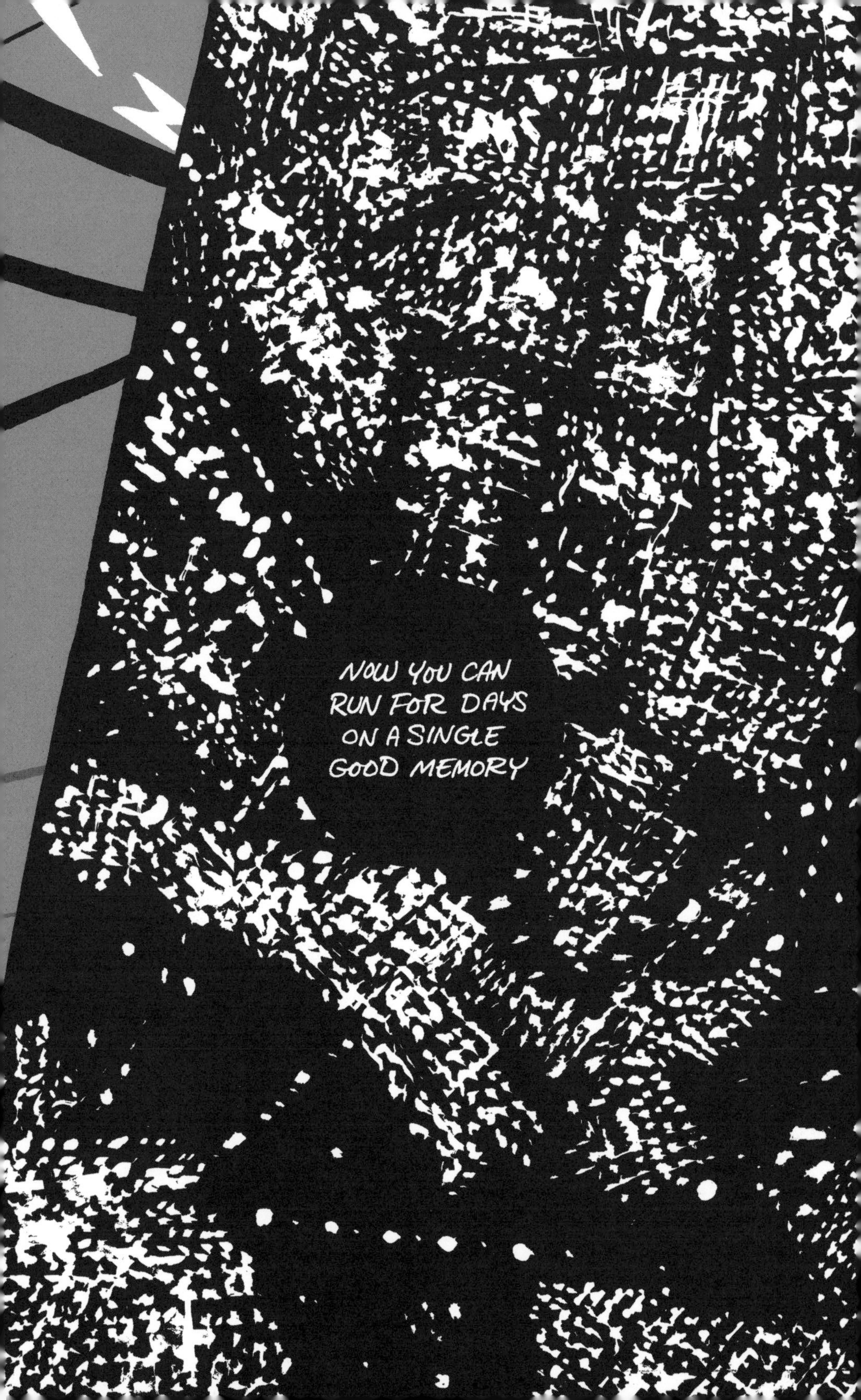
NOW YOU CAN RUN FOR DAYS ON A SINGLE GOOD MEMORY

AND
YOU CAN GIVE
THIS HAPPINESS
TO OTHERS

SEVENTH ENERGY

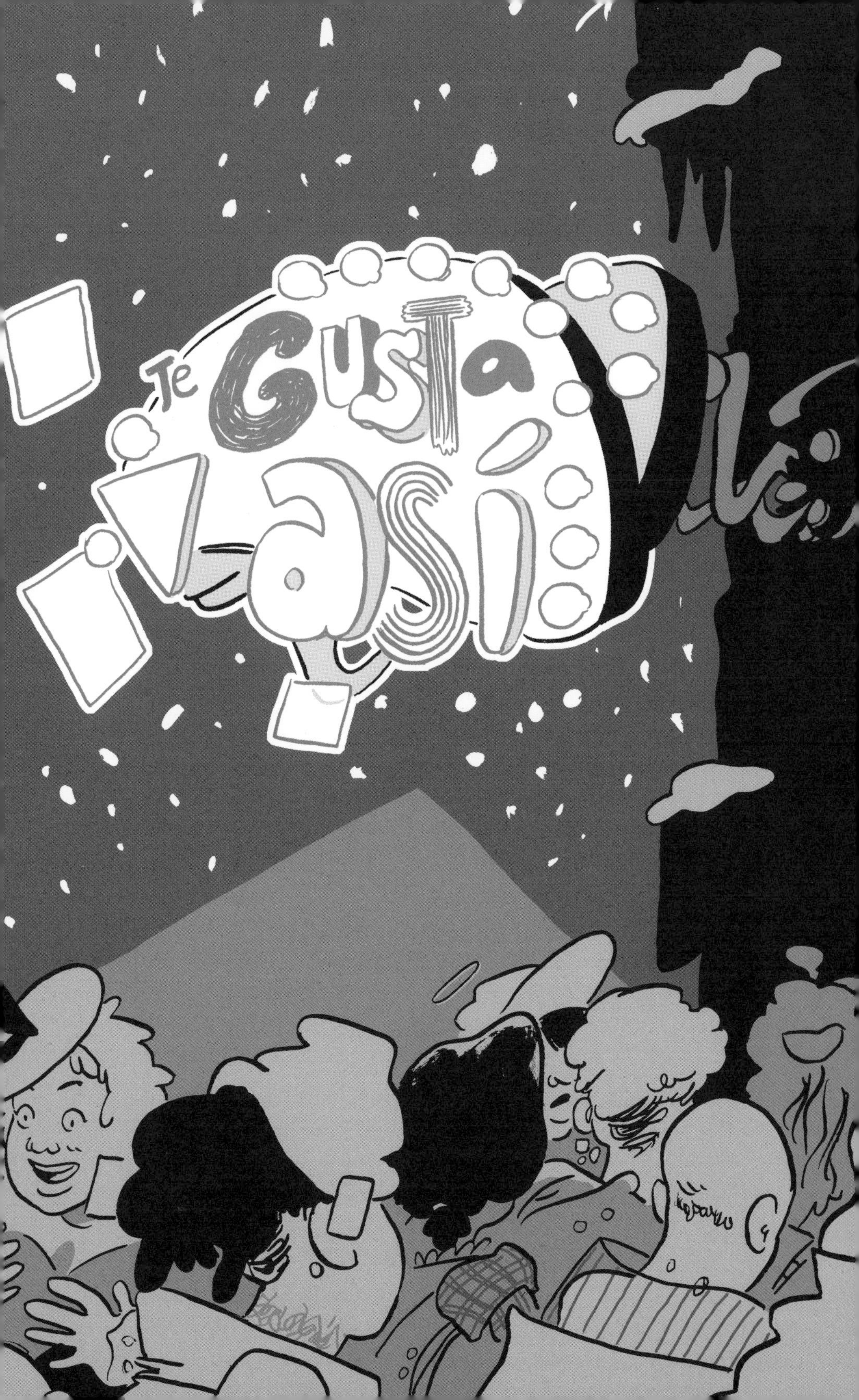
Te Gusta así

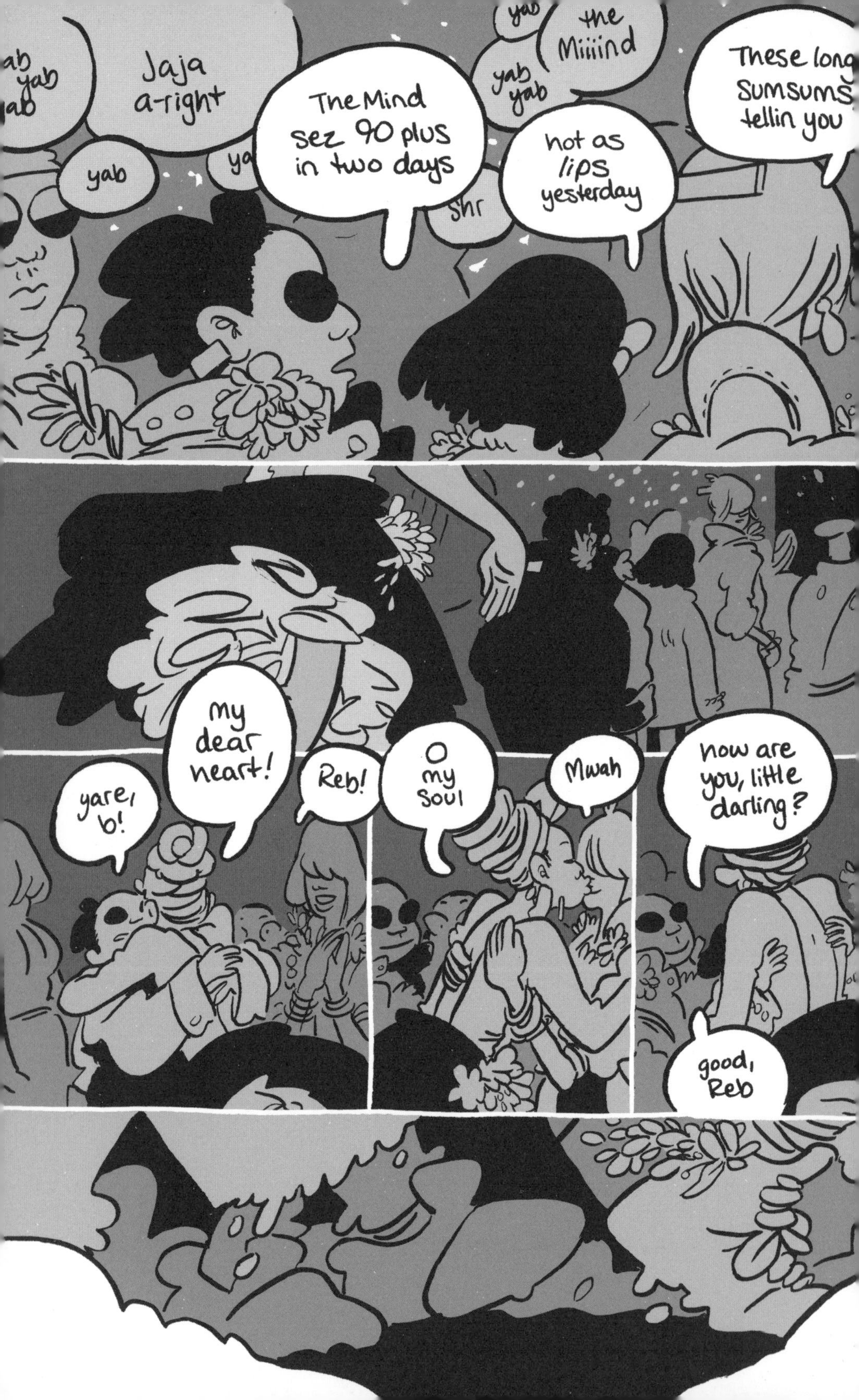
yab yab yab
Jaja a-right
yab
ya
The Mind sez 90 plus in two days
yab
the Miiiind
yab yab
hot as lips yesterday
shr
These long sumsums tellin you
yare, b!
my dear heart!
Reb!
O my soul
Mwah
how are you, little darling?
good, Reb

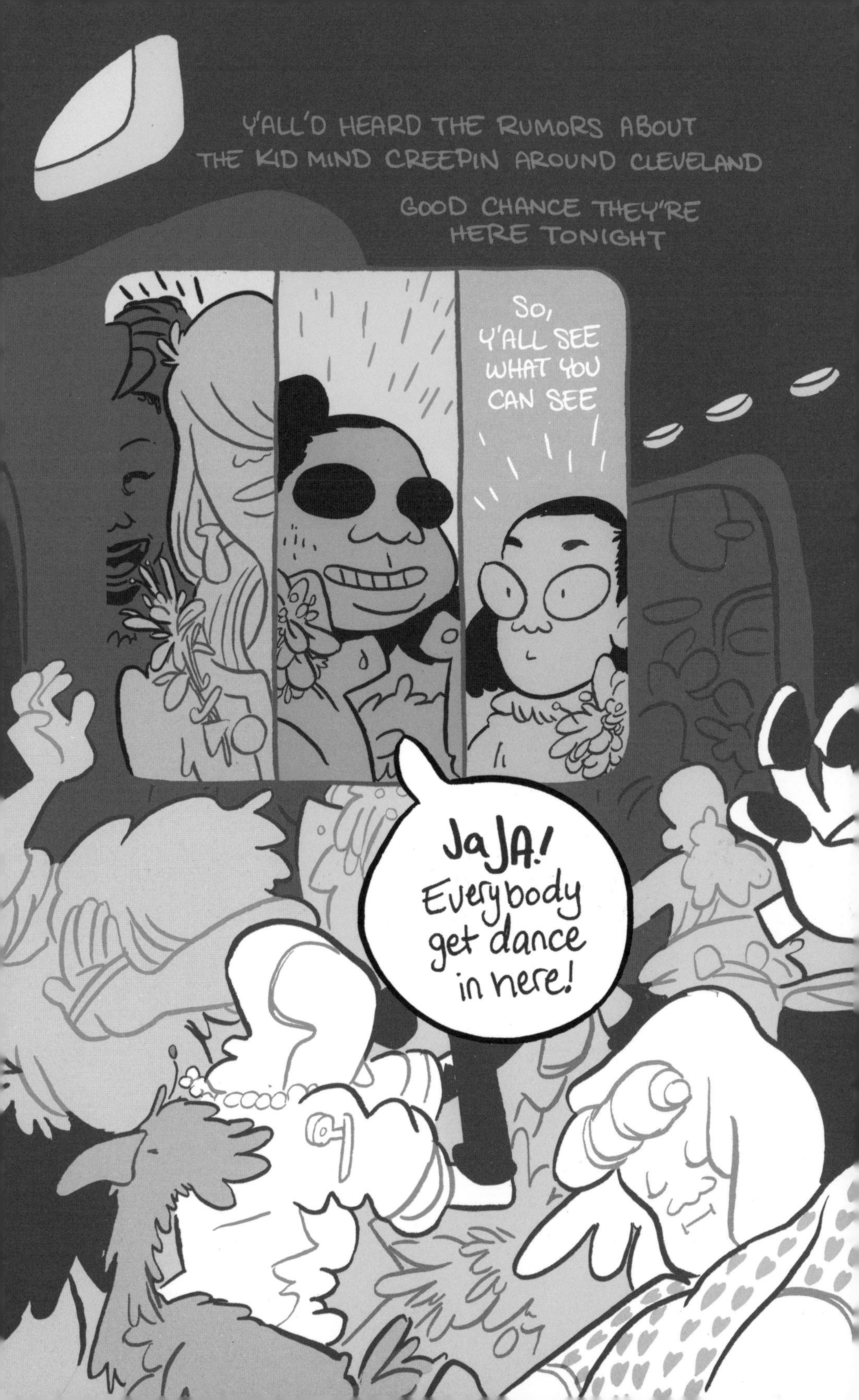
Y'ALL'D HEARD THE RUMORS ABOUT THE KID MIND CREEPIN AROUND CLEVELAND
GOOD CHANCE THEY'RE HERE TONIGHT
So, Y'ALL SEE WHAT YOU CAN SEE
JaJA! Everybody get dance in here!

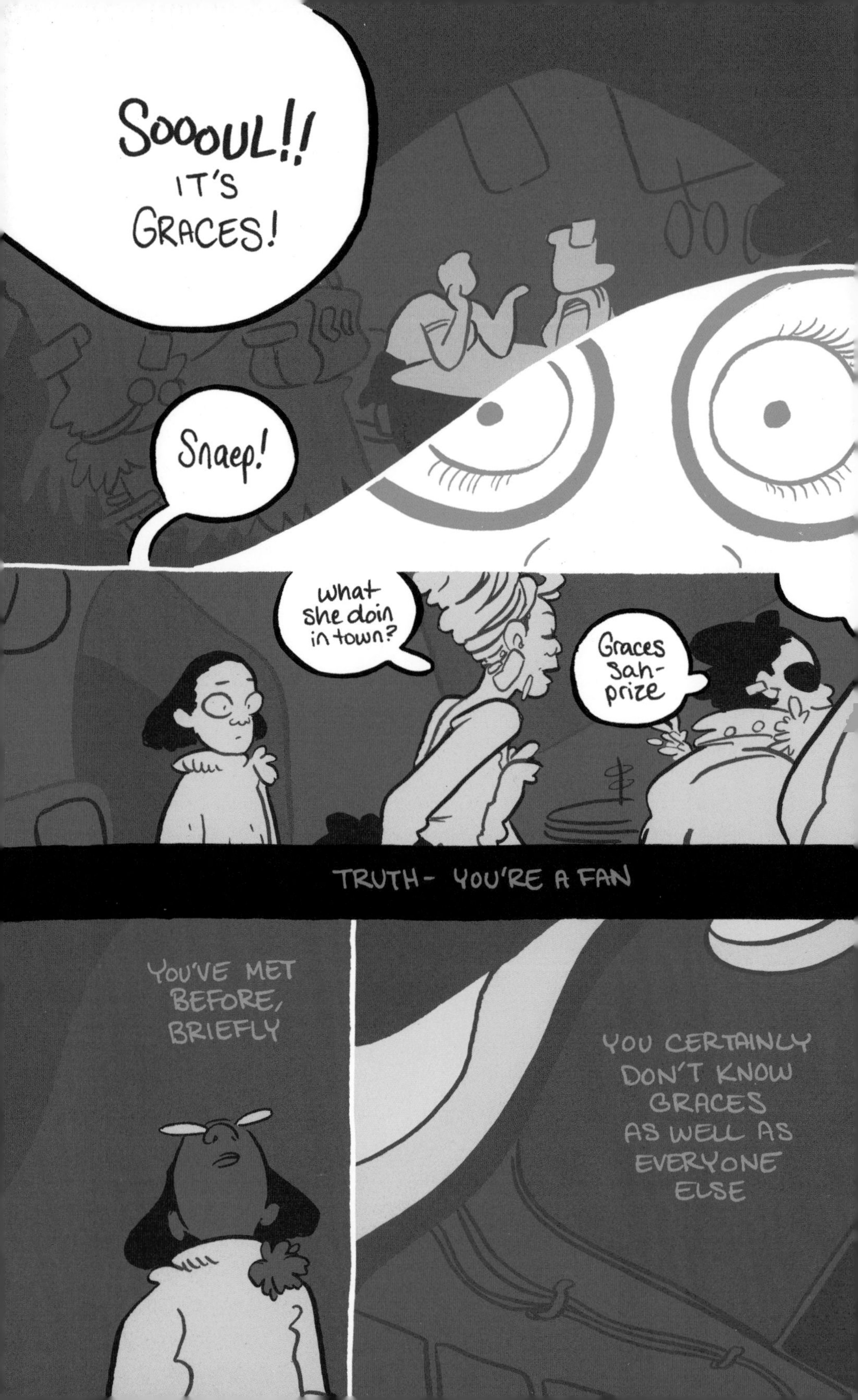
SOOOUL!!
IT'S
GRACES!
Snaep!
what
she doin
in town?
Graces
Sah-
prize
TRUTH- YOU'RE A FAN
YOU'VE MET
BEFORE,
BRIEFLY
YOU CERTAINLY
DON'T KNOW
GRACES
AS WELL AS
EVERYONE
ELSE

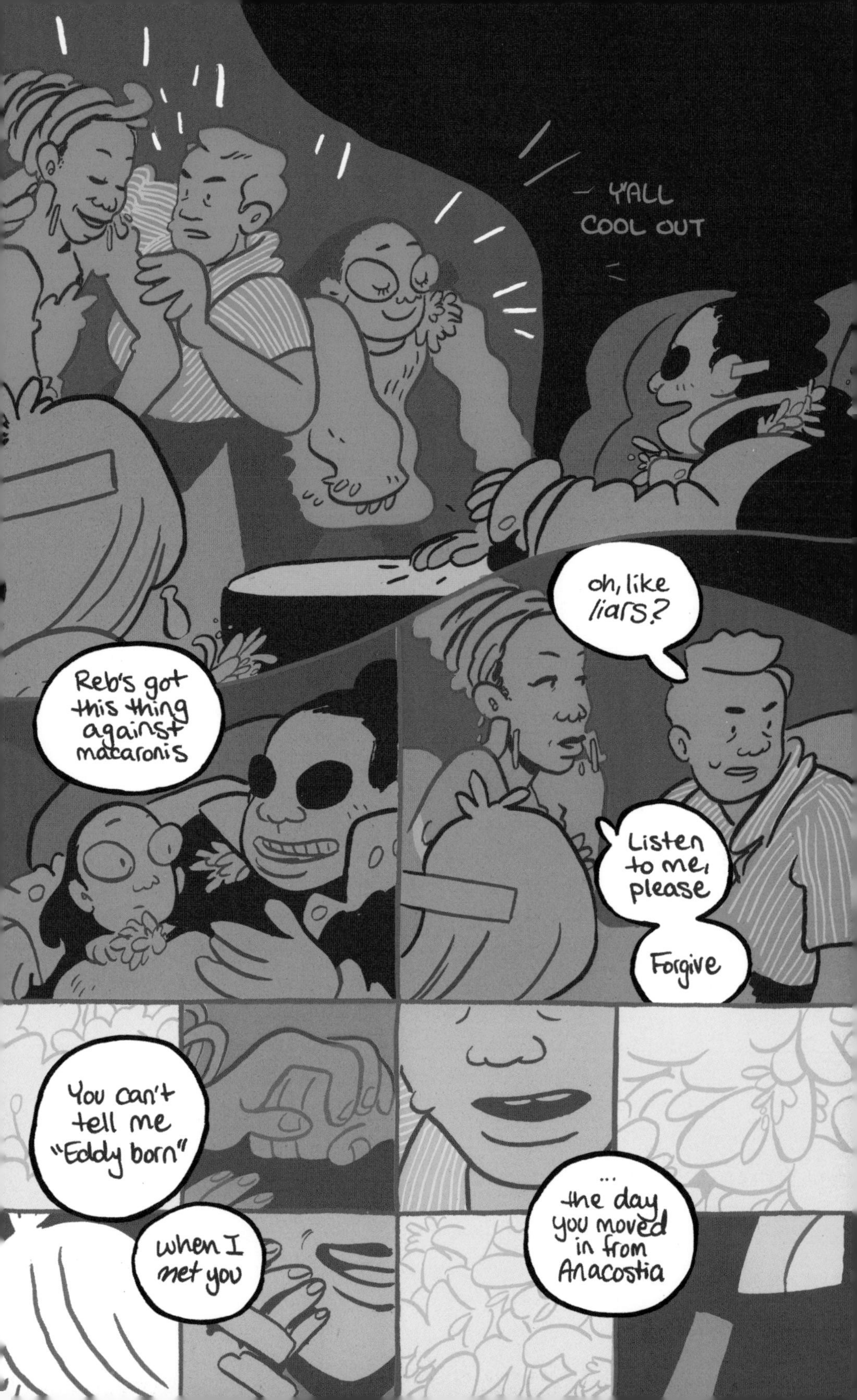
Y'ALL
COOL OUT
Reb's got this thing against macaronis
oh, like liars?
Listen to me, please
Forgive
You can't tell me "Eddy born"
when I met you
... the day you moved in from Anacostia

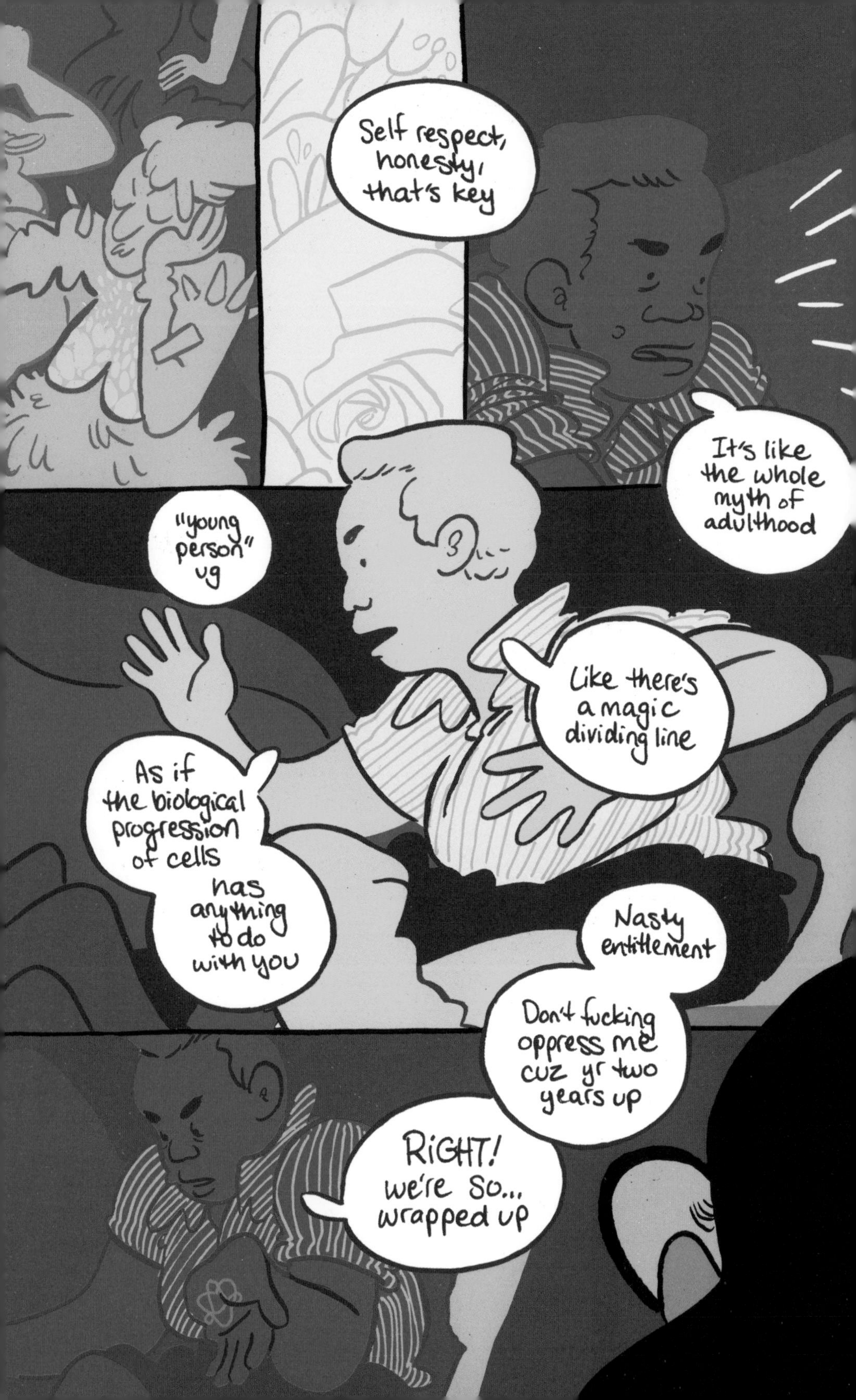
Self respect, honesty, that's key
It's like the whole myth of adulthood
"young person" ug
Like there's a magic dividing line
As if the biological progression of cells
has anything to do with you
Nasty entitlement
Don't fucking oppress me cuz yr two years up
RIGHT! we're so... wrapped up

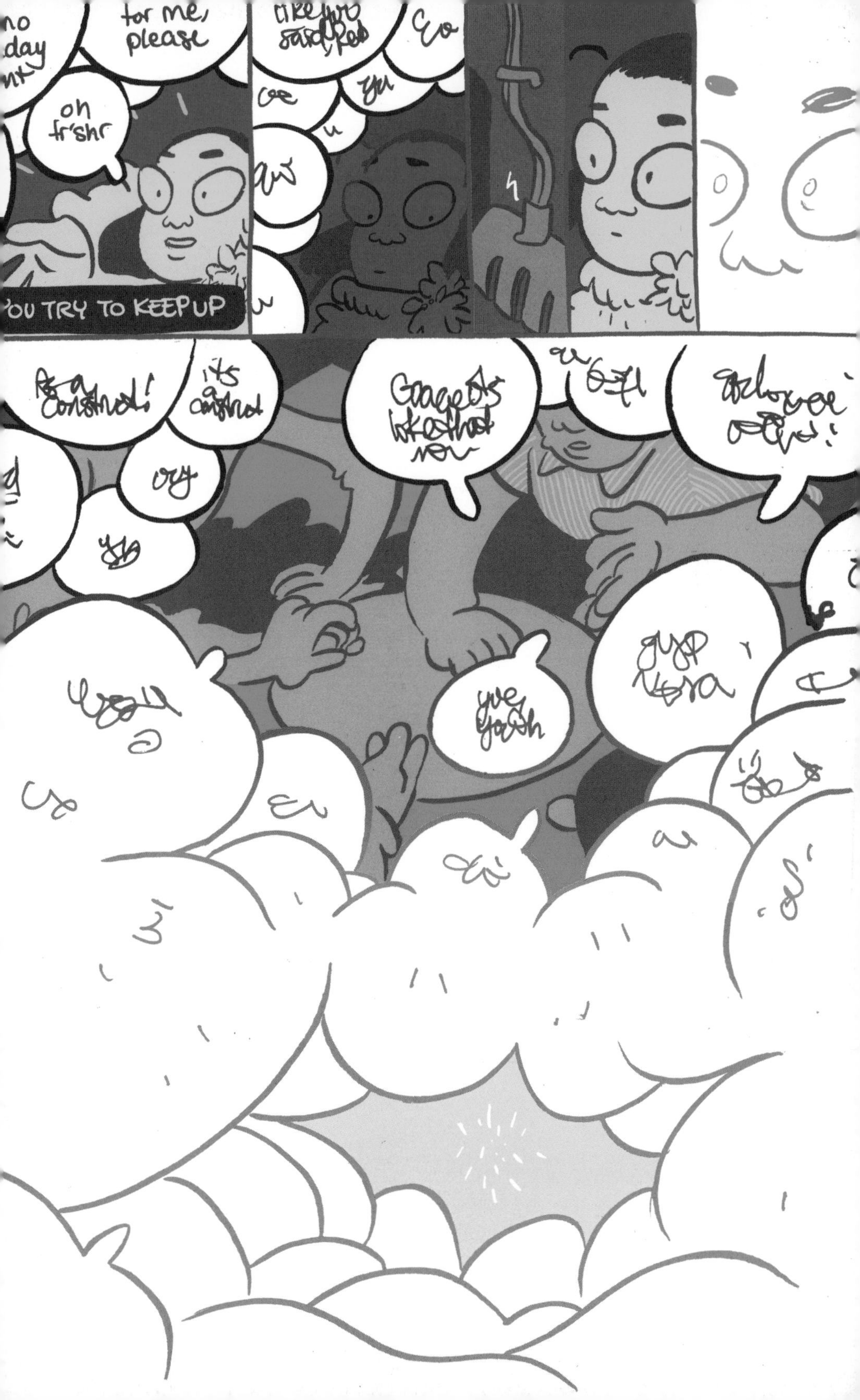
for me,
please
oh
fr'shr
YOU TRY TO KEEP UP

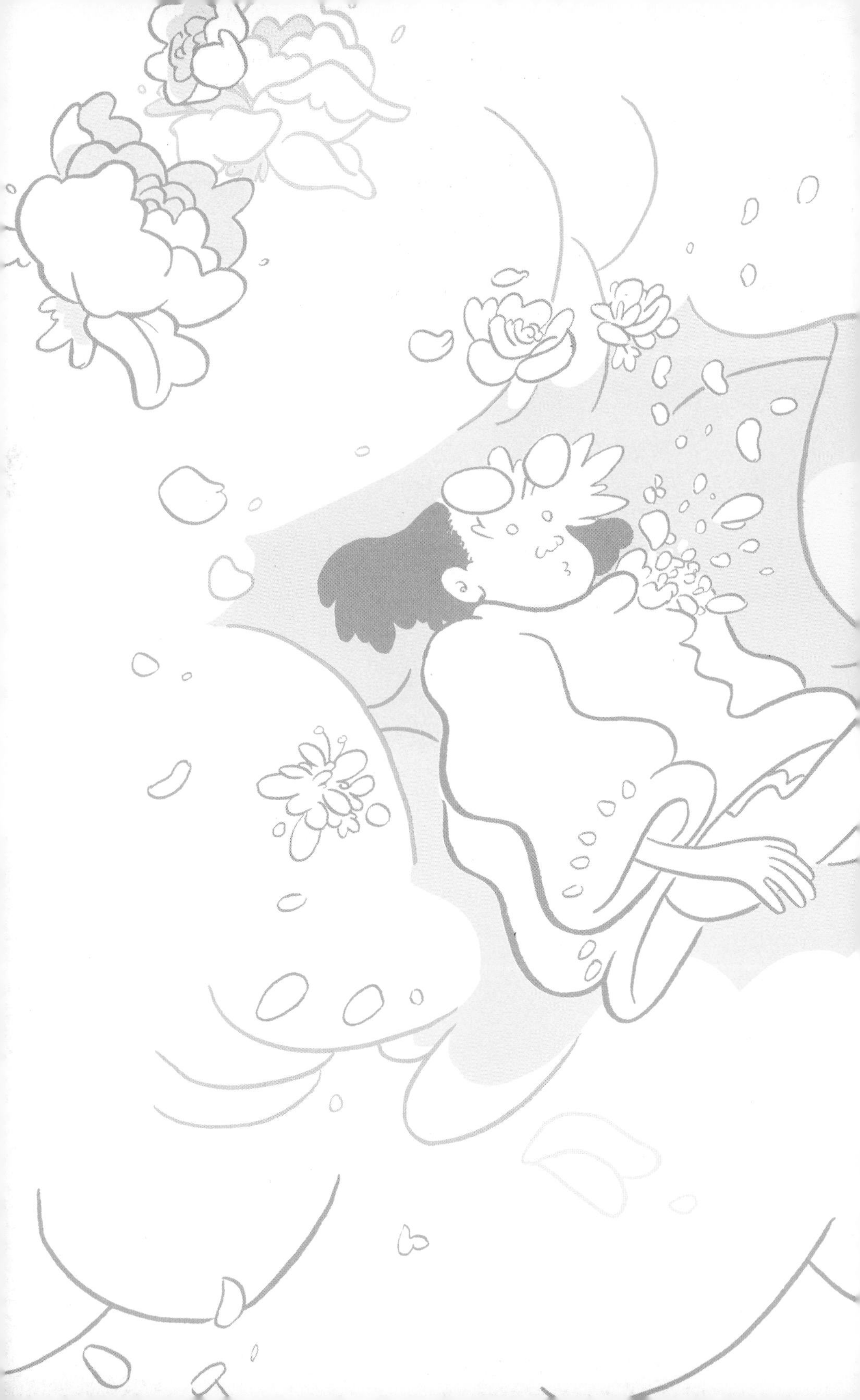

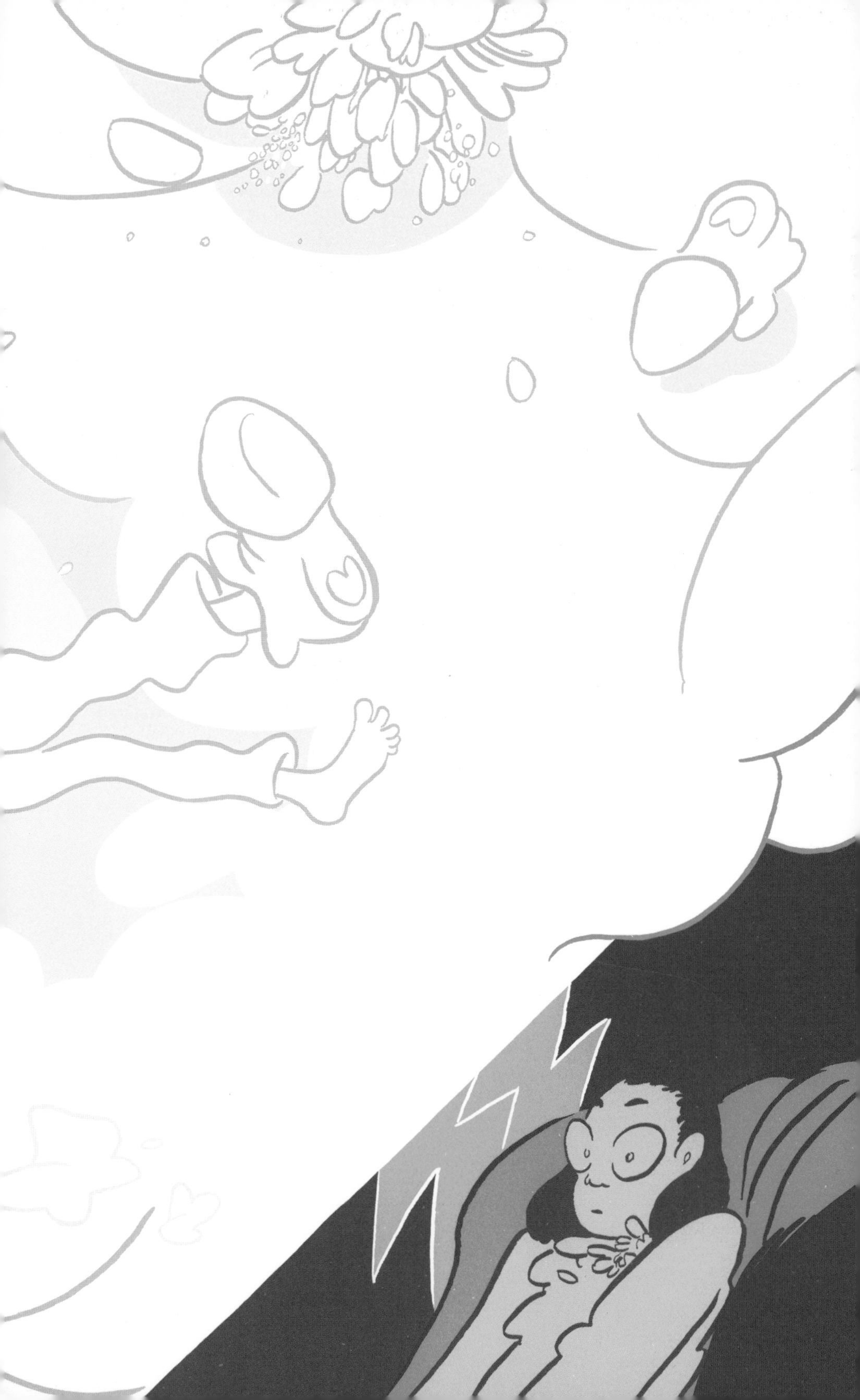

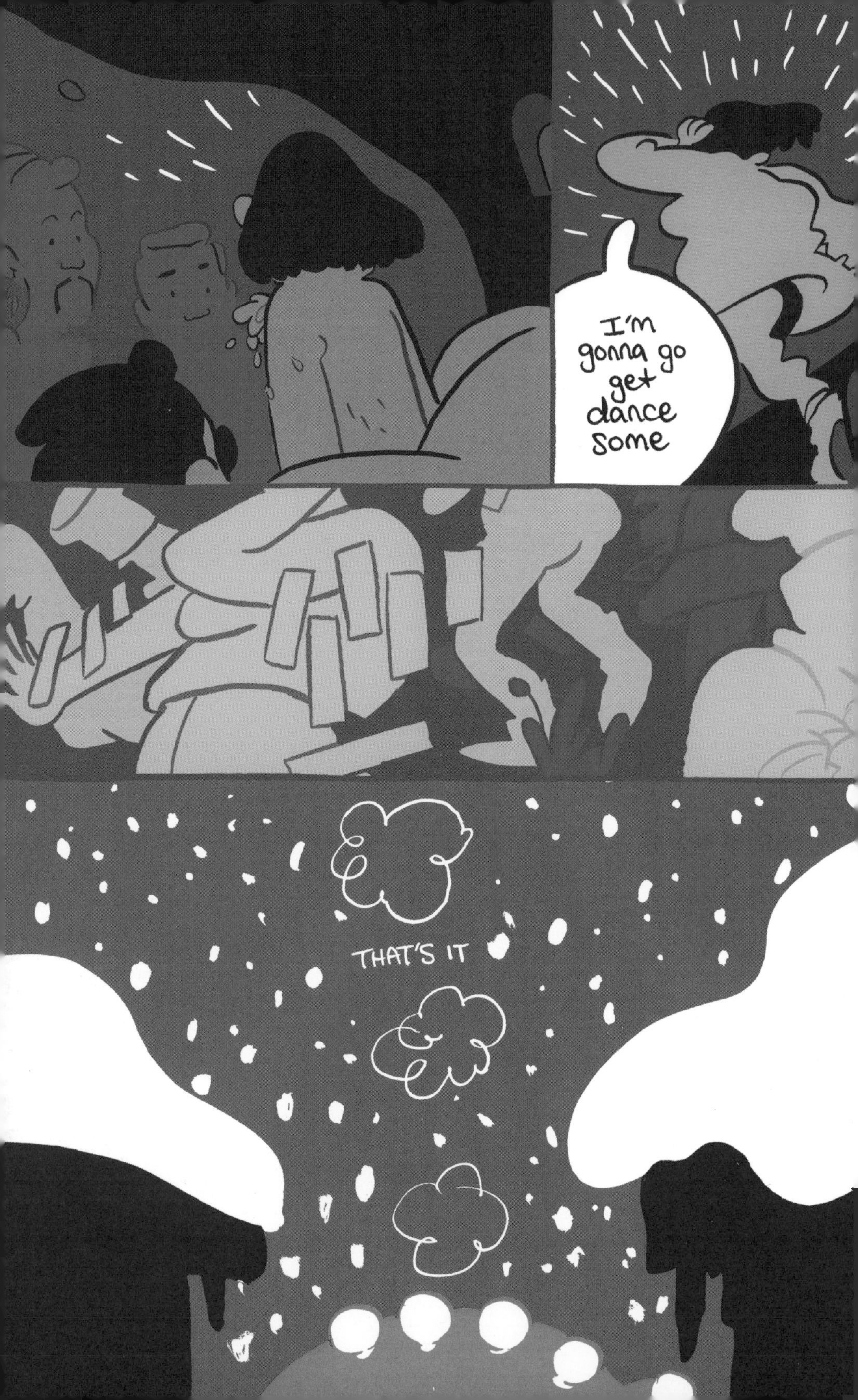
I'm gonna go get dance some
THAT'S IT

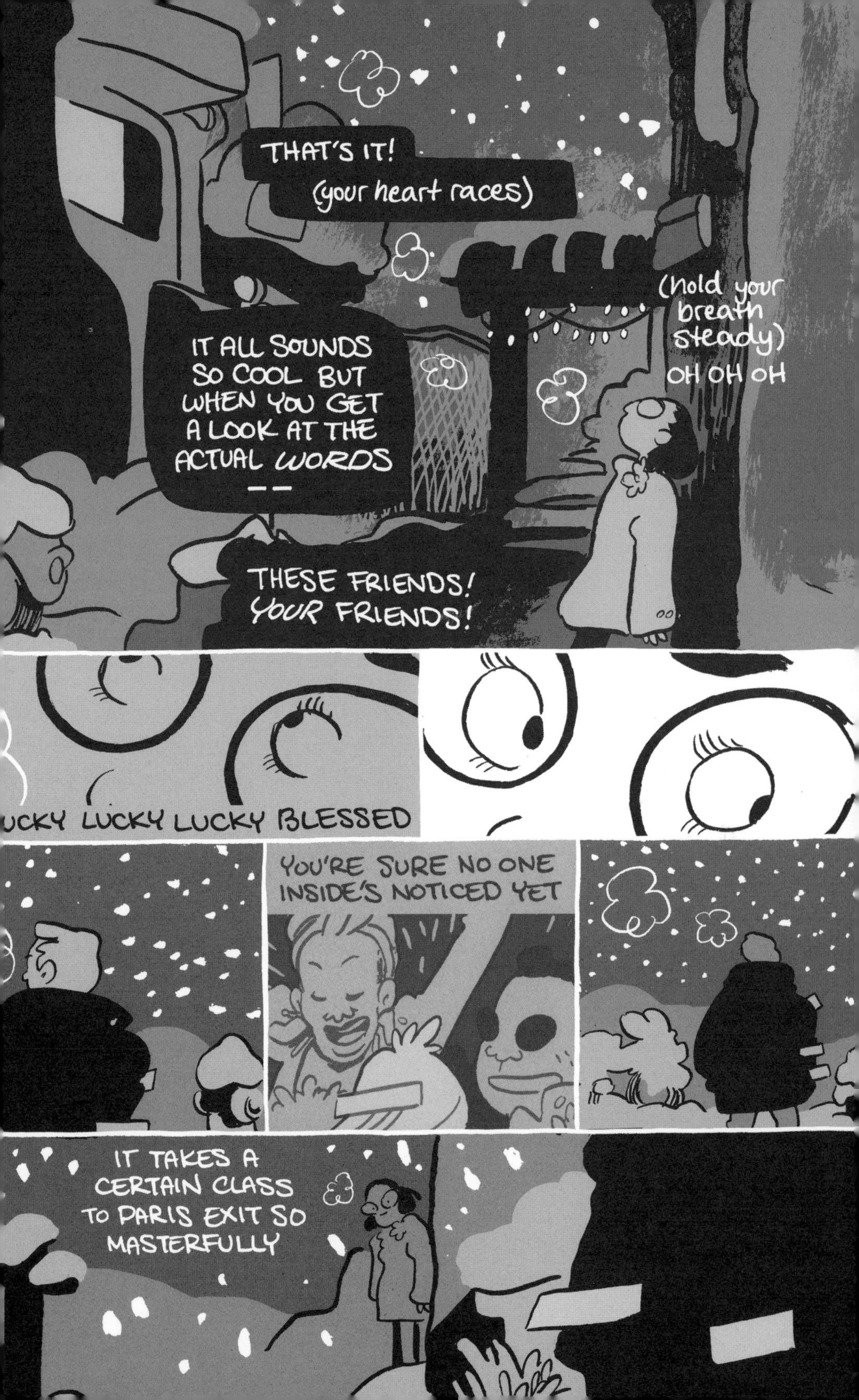
THAT'S IT!
(your heart races)
IT ALL SOUNDS SO COOL BUT WHEN YOU GET A LOOK AT THE ACTUAL *WORDS* --
(hold your breath steady)
OH OH OH
THESE FRIENDS! *YOUR* FRIENDS!
UCKY LUCKY LUCKY BLESSED
YOU'RE SURE NO ONE INSIDE'S NOTICED YET
IT TAKES A CERTAIN CLASS TO PARIS EXIT SO MASTERFULLY

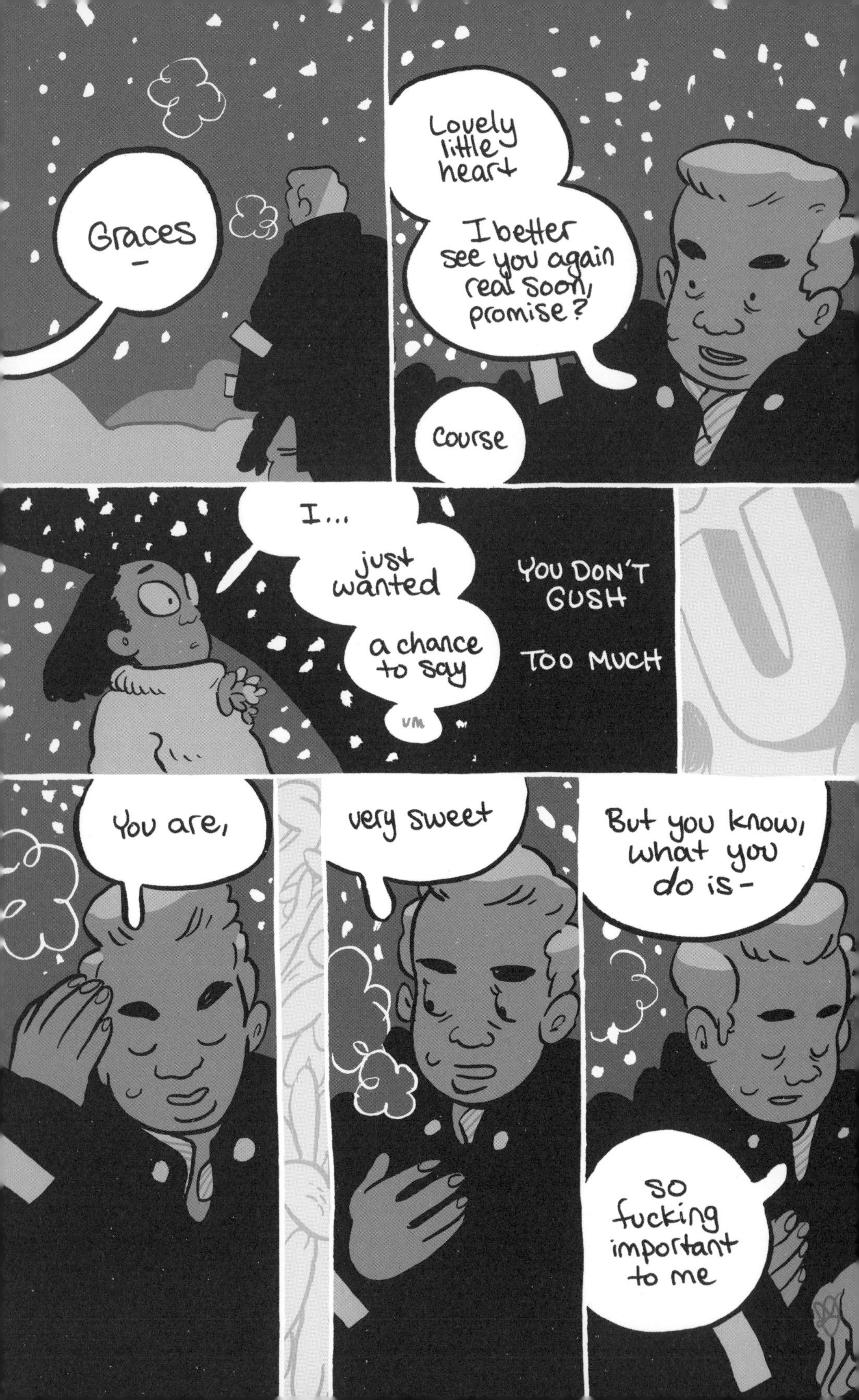
Graces -
Lovely little heart
I better see you again real soon, promise?
Course
I...
just wanted
a chance to say
um
YOU DON'T GUSH
TOO MUCH
You are,
very sweet
But you know, what you do is -
so fucking important to me

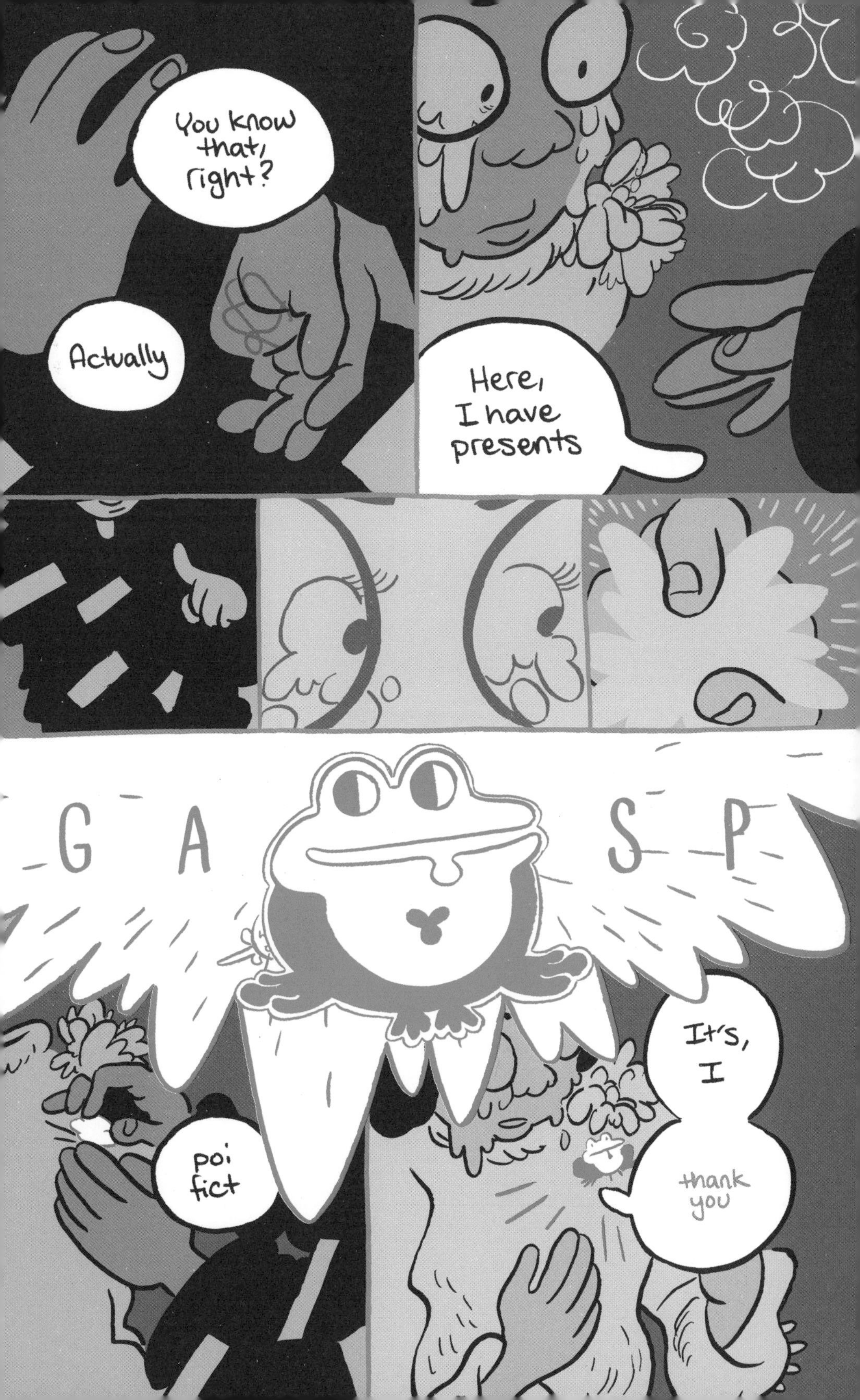
You know that, right?
Actually
Here, I have presents
GASP
It's, I
poi fict
thank you

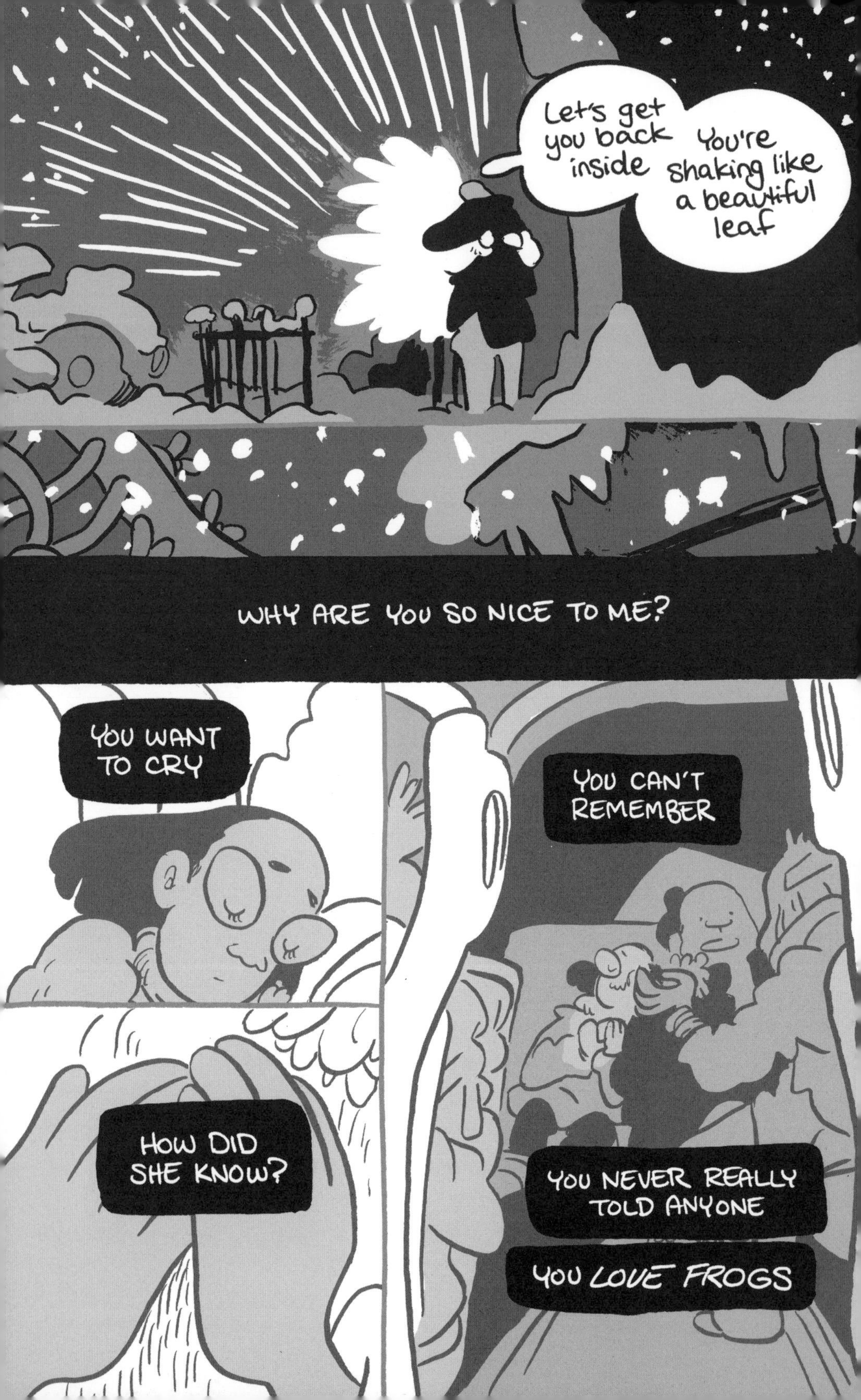
Let's get you back inside
You're shaking like a beautiful leaf
WHY ARE YOU SO NICE TO ME?
YOU WANT TO CRY
YOU CAN'T REMEMBER
HOW DID SHE KNOW?
YOU NEVER REALLY TOLD ANYONE
YOU LOVE FROGS

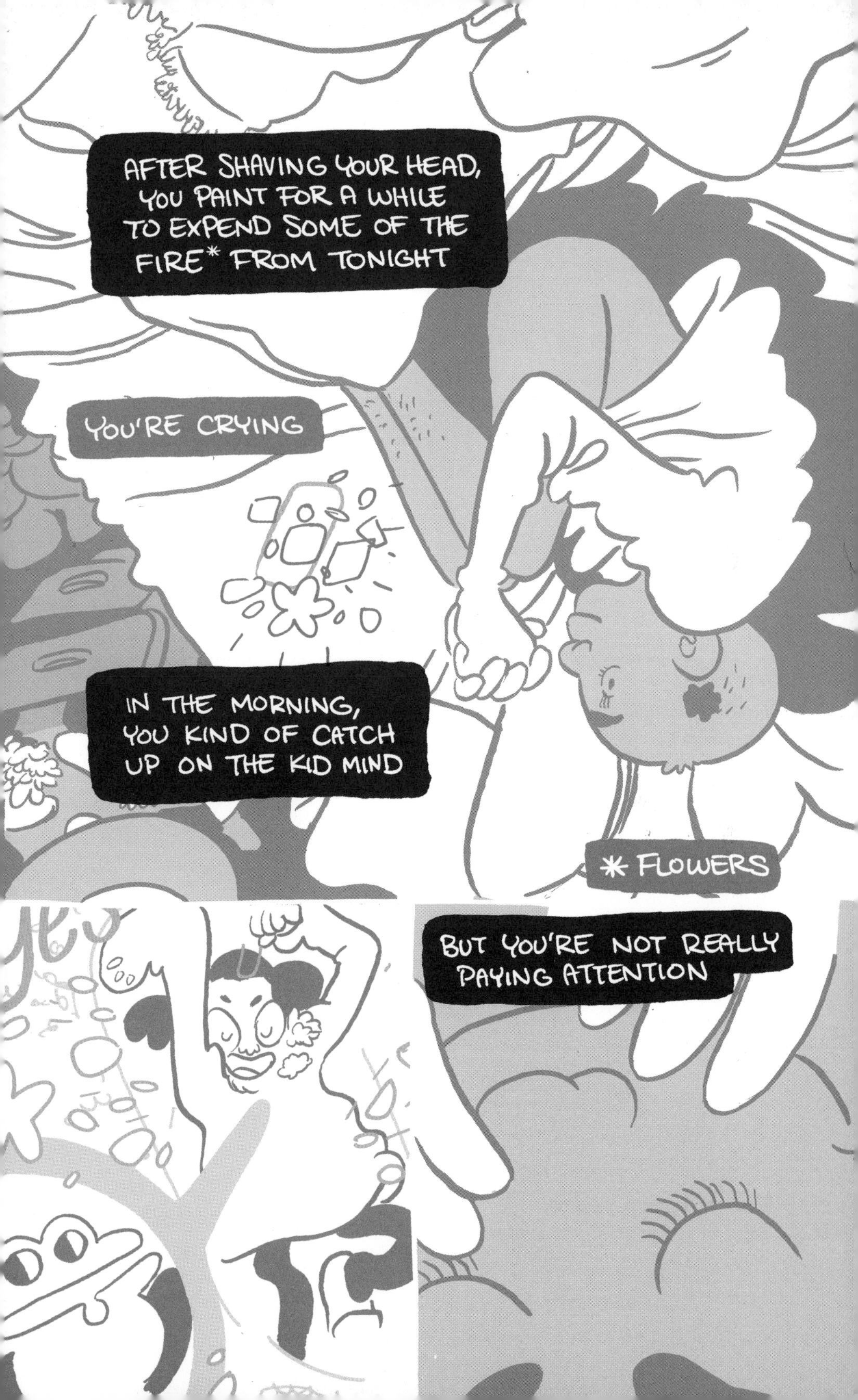
AFTER SHAVING YOUR HEAD, YOU PAINT FOR A WHILE TO EXPEND SOME OF THE FIRE* FROM TONIGHT
YOU'RE CRYING
IN THE MORNING, YOU KIND OF CATCH UP ON THE KID MIND
* FLOWERS
BUT YOU'RE NOT REALLY PAYING ATTENTION

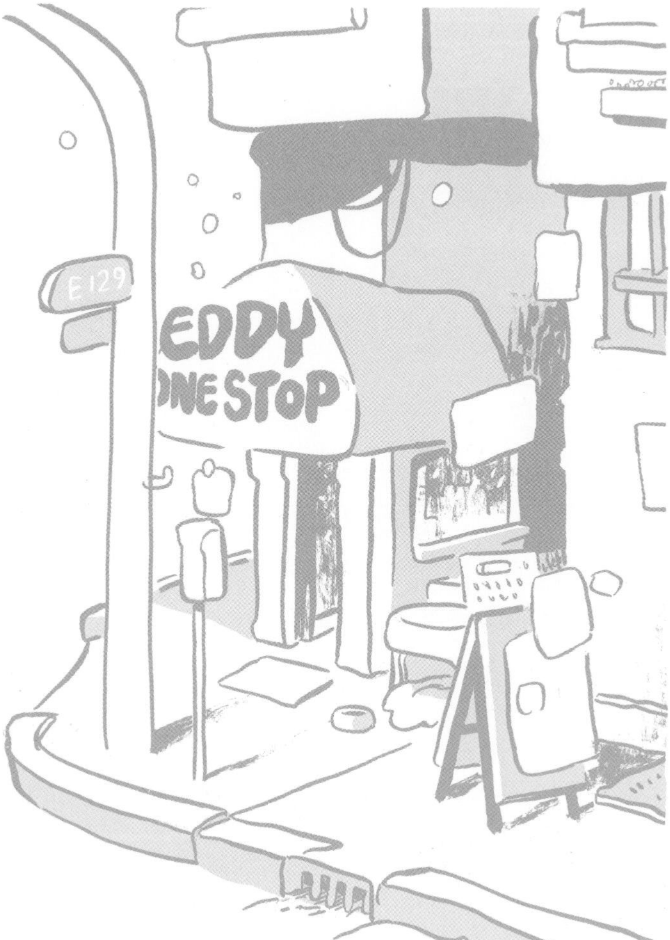
E129
EDDY
STOP

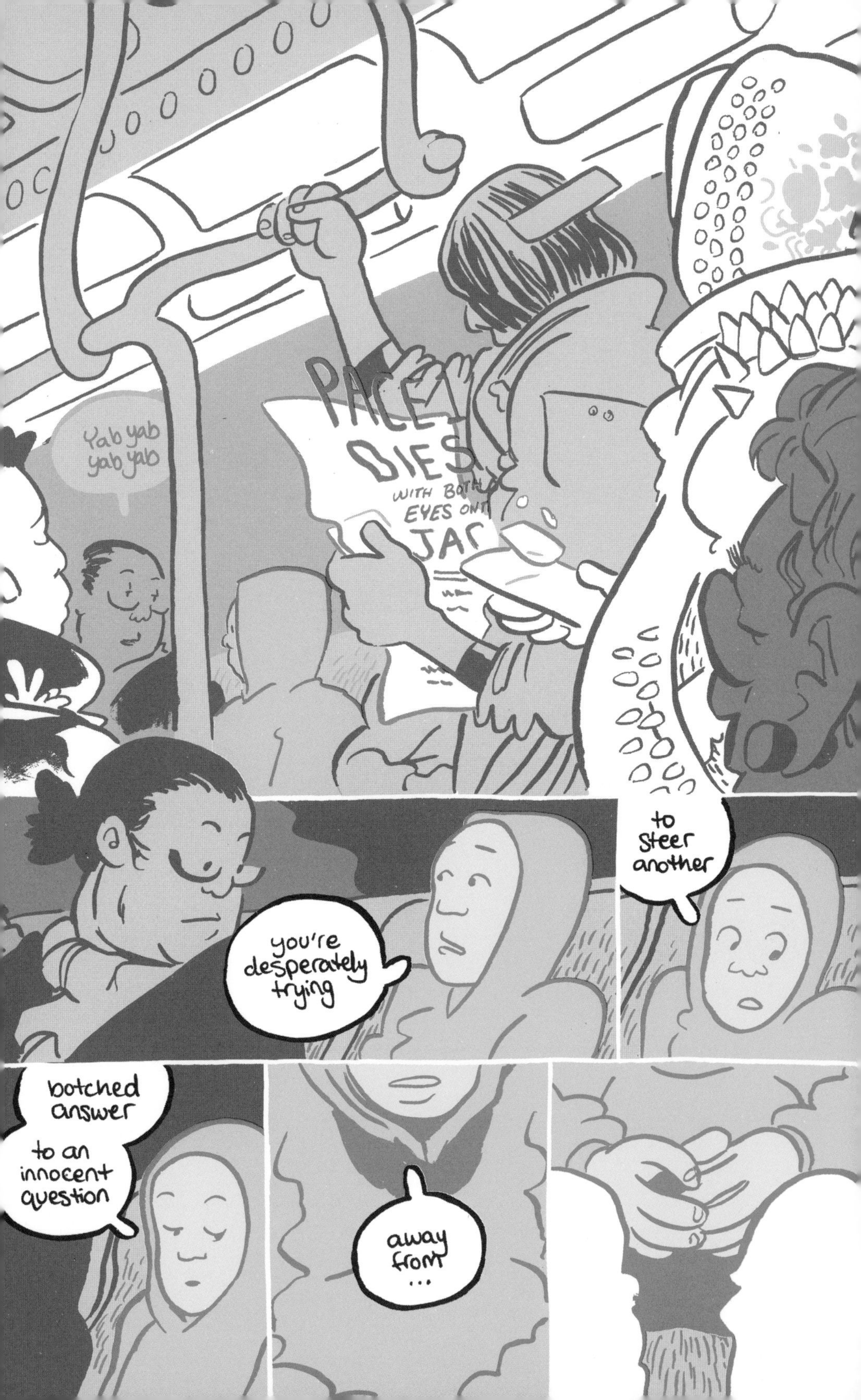
PACE
DIES
WITH BOTH EYES ON
JAC
Yab yab yab yab
you're desperately trying
to steer another
botched answer
to an innocent question
away from ...

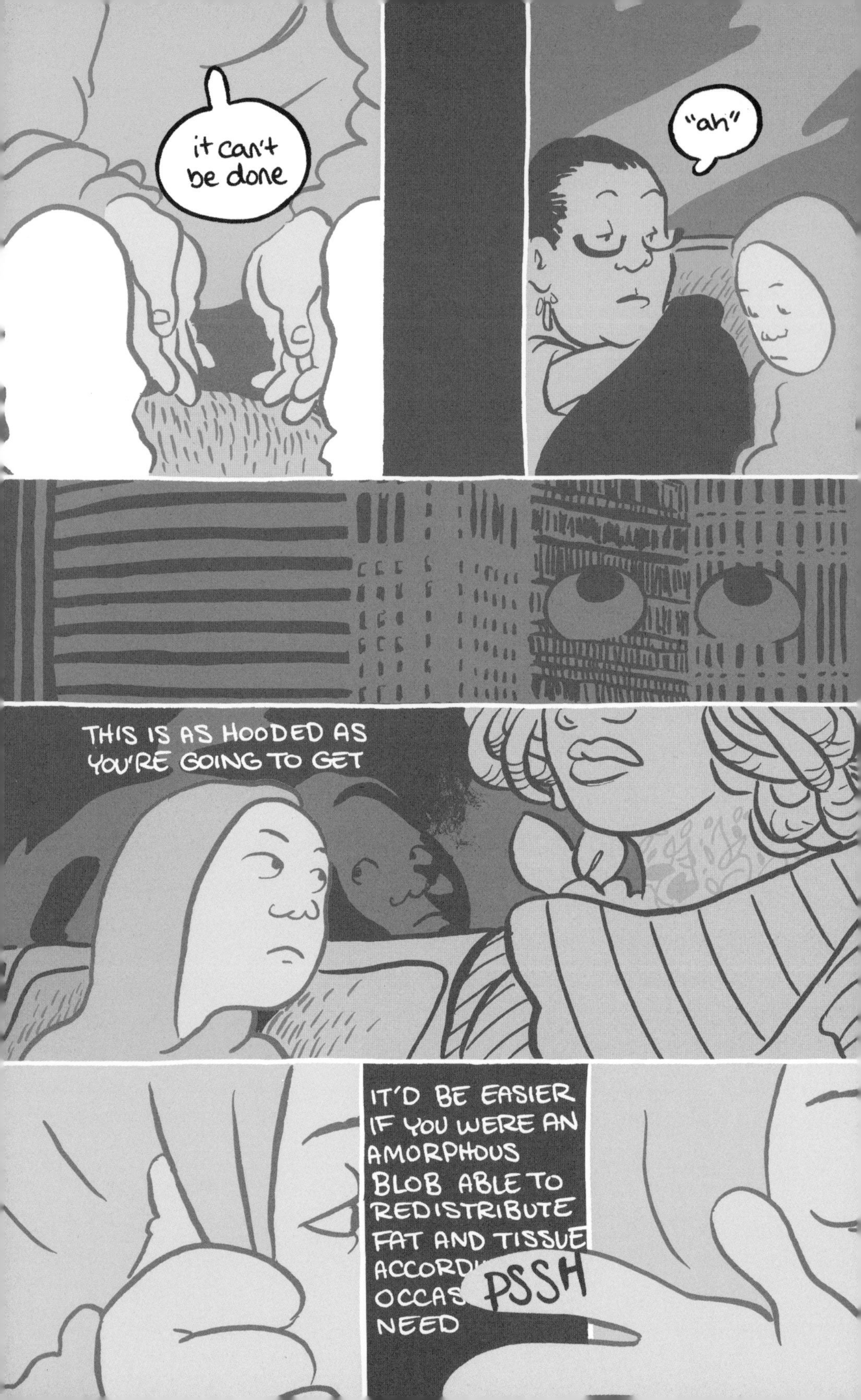
it can't be done
"ah"
THIS IS AS HOODED AS YOU'RE GOING TO GET
IT'D BE EASIER IF YOU WERE AN AMORPHOUS BLOB ABLE TO REDISTRIBUTE FAT AND TISSUE ACCORD
OCCAS
NEED
PSSH

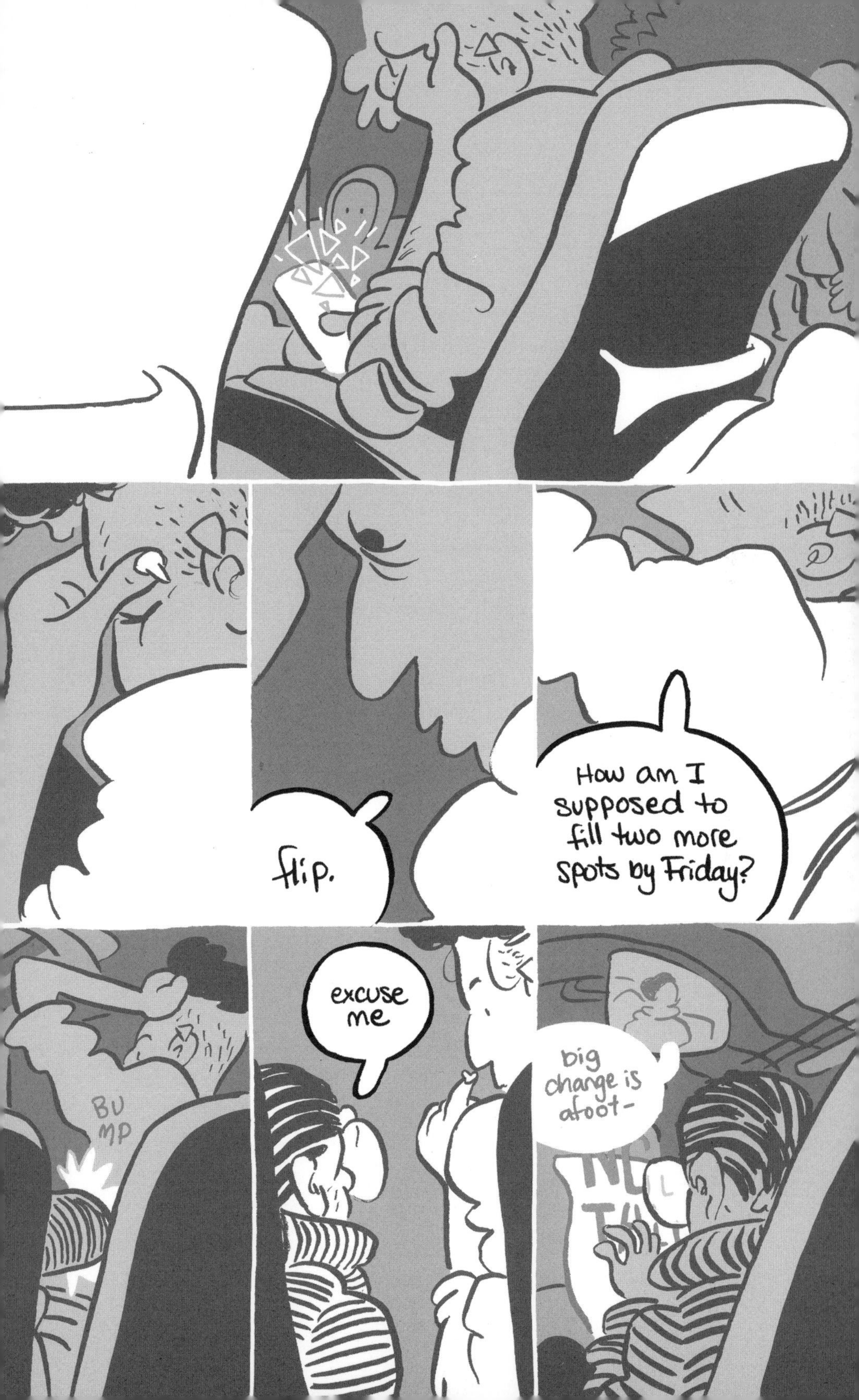
flip.
How am I supposed to fill two more spots by Friday?
BUMP
excuse me
big change is afoot-

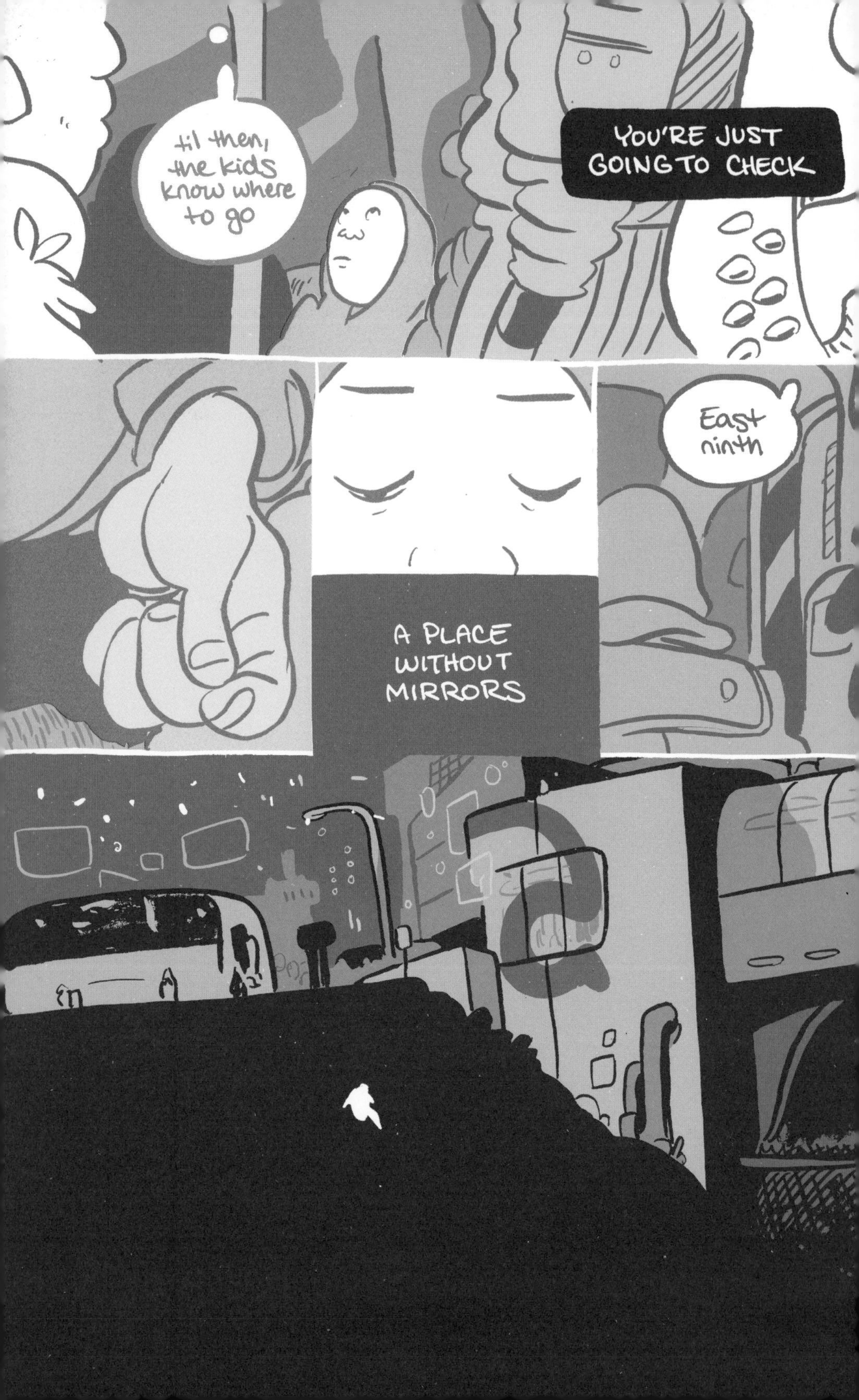
til then, the kids know where to go
YOU'RE JUST GOING TO CHECK
East ninth
A PLACE WITHOUT MIRRORS

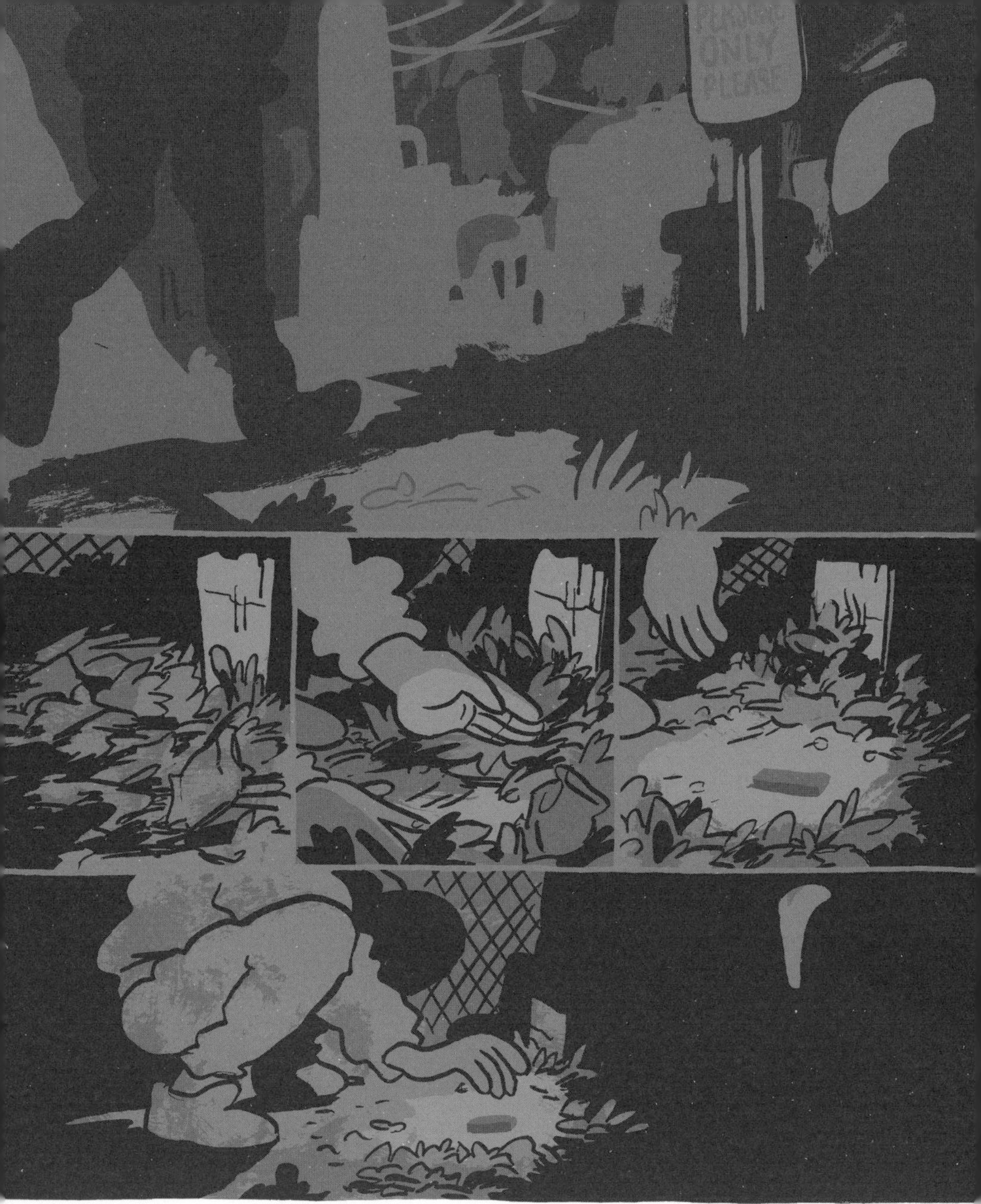
ONLY
PLEASE

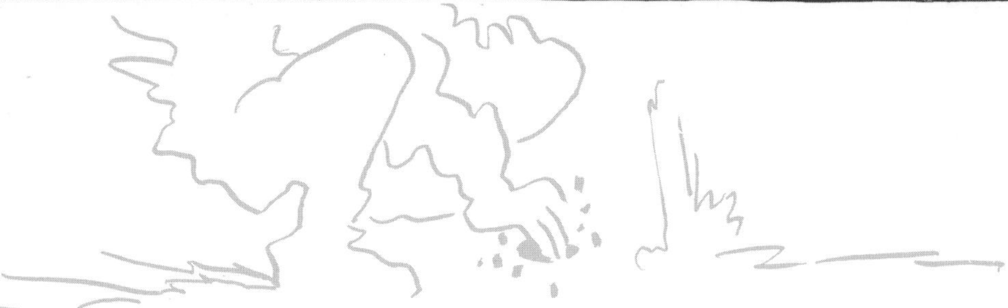

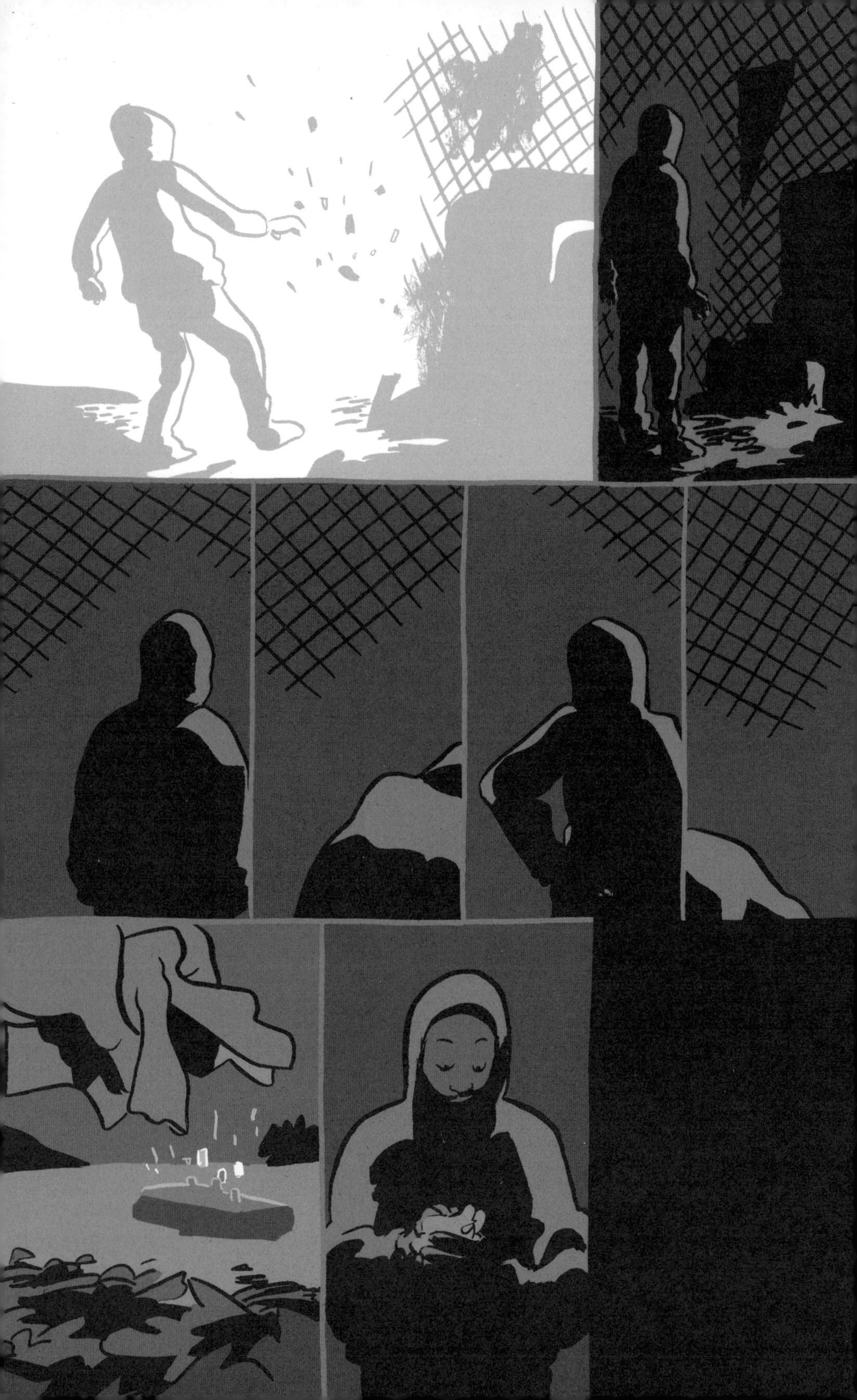

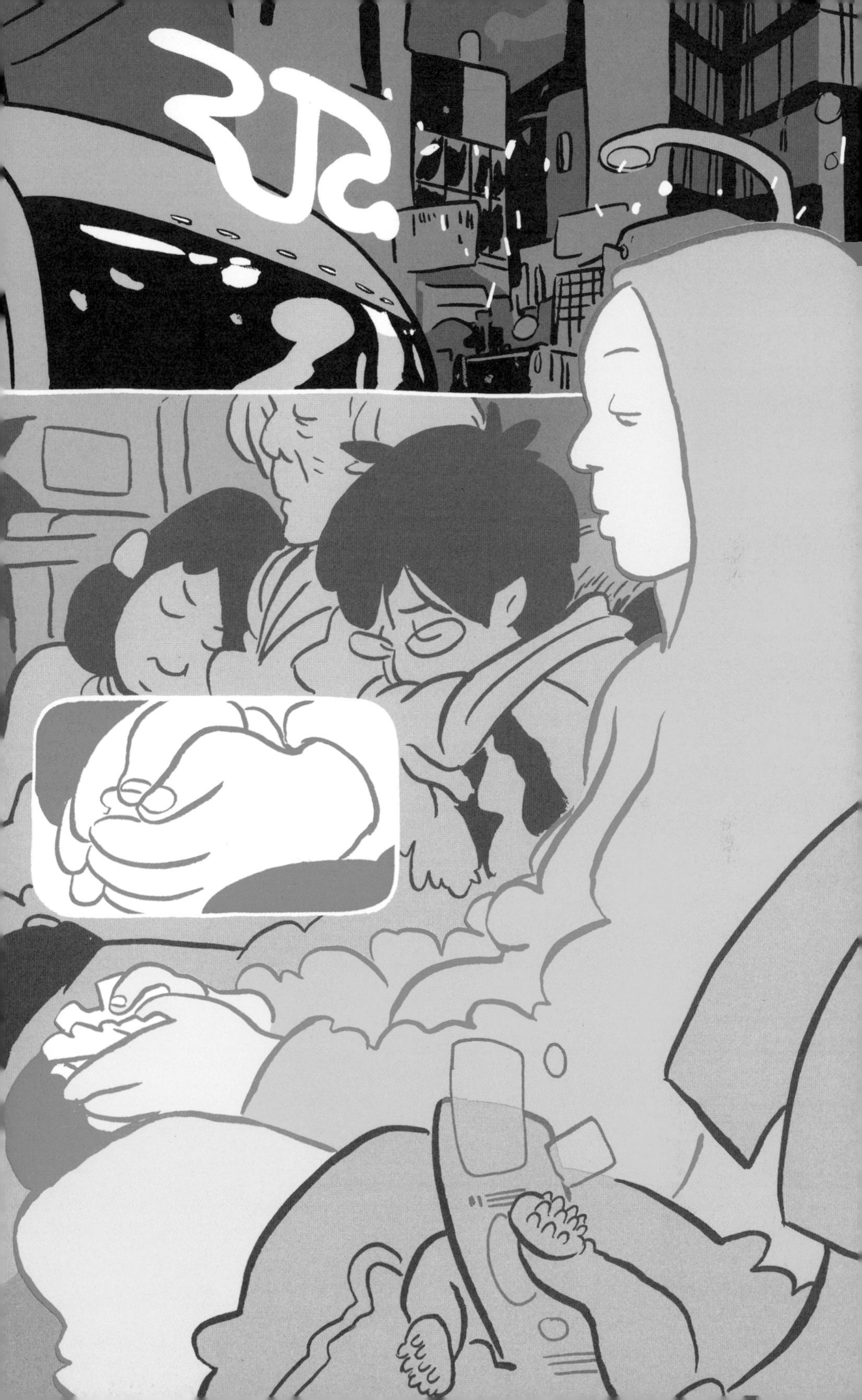

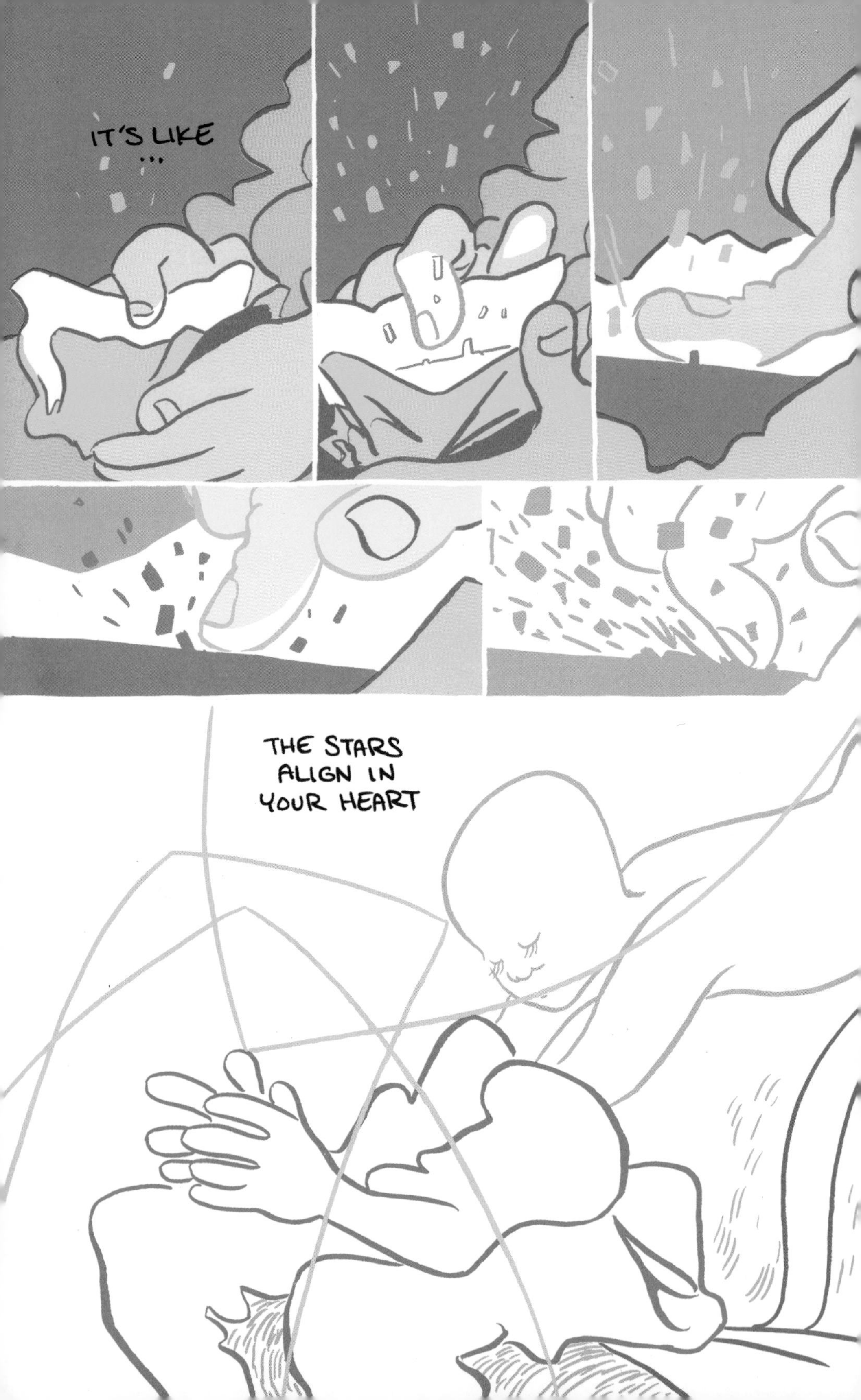
IT'S LIKE
...
THE STARS ALIGN IN YOUR HEART

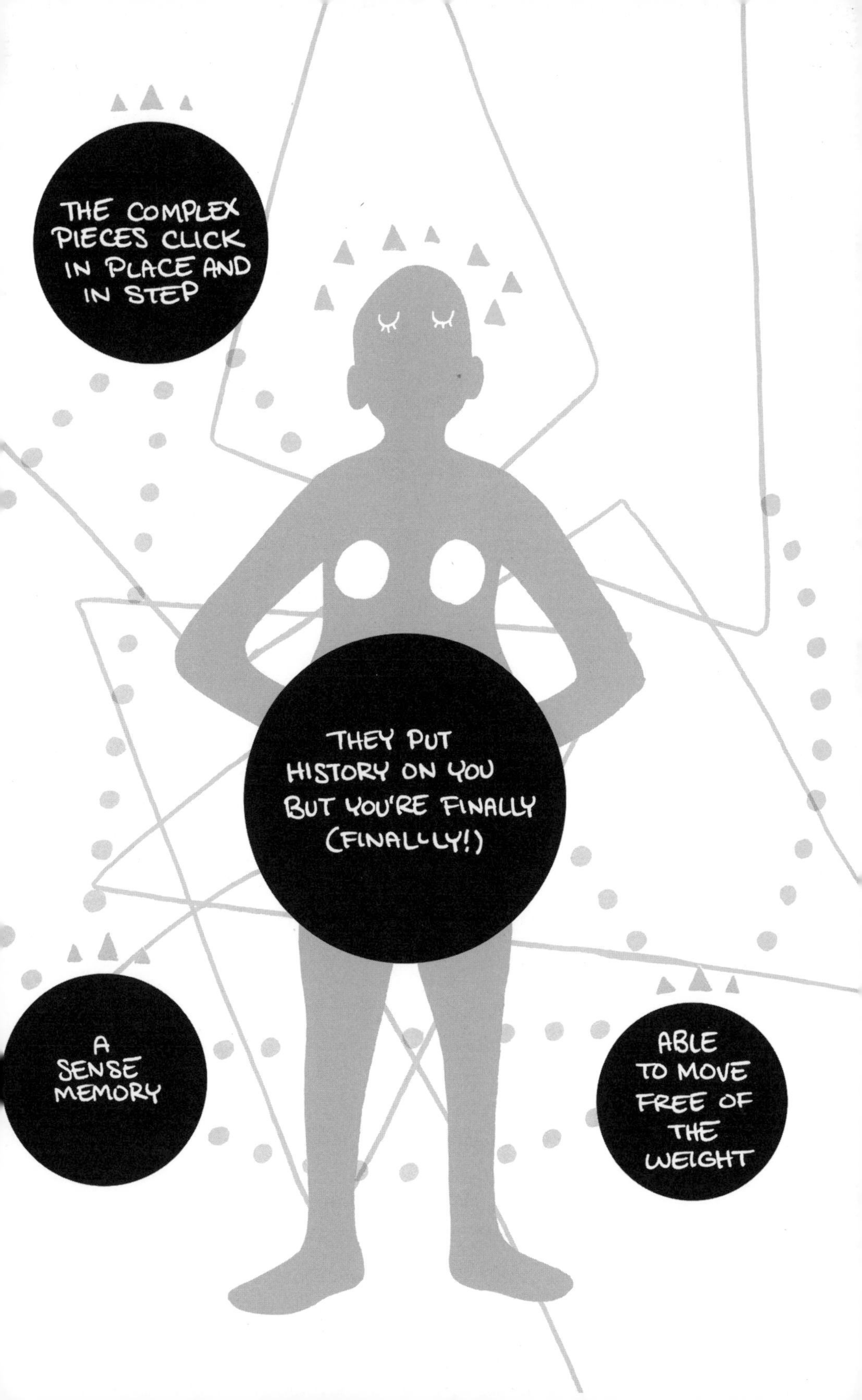
THE COMPLEX PIECES CLICK IN PLACE AND IN STEP
THEY PUT HISTORY ON YOU BUT YOU'RE FINALLY (FINALLLY!)
A SENSE MEMORY
ABLE TO MOVE FREE OF THE WEIGHT

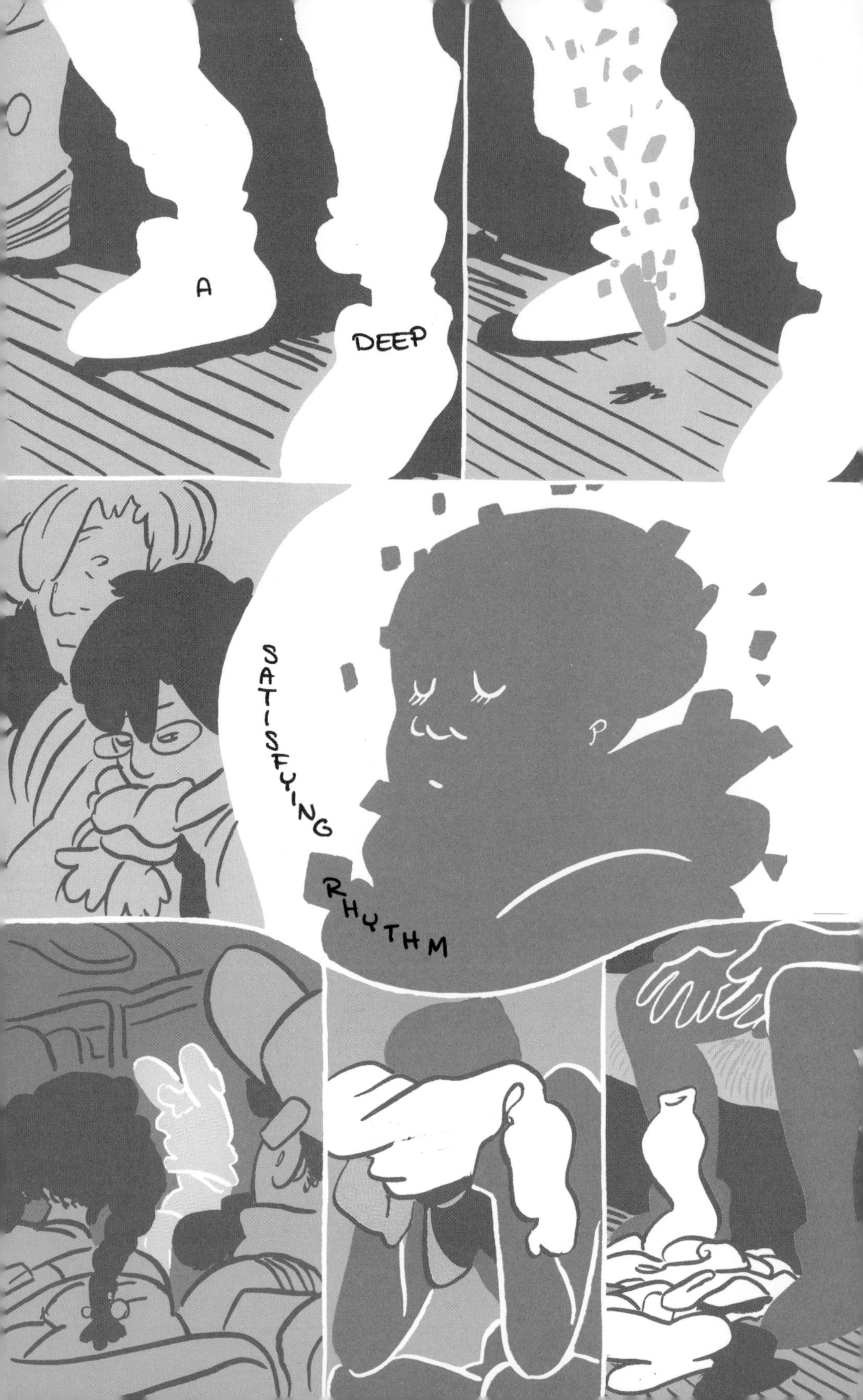
A
DEEP
SATISFYING
RHYTHM

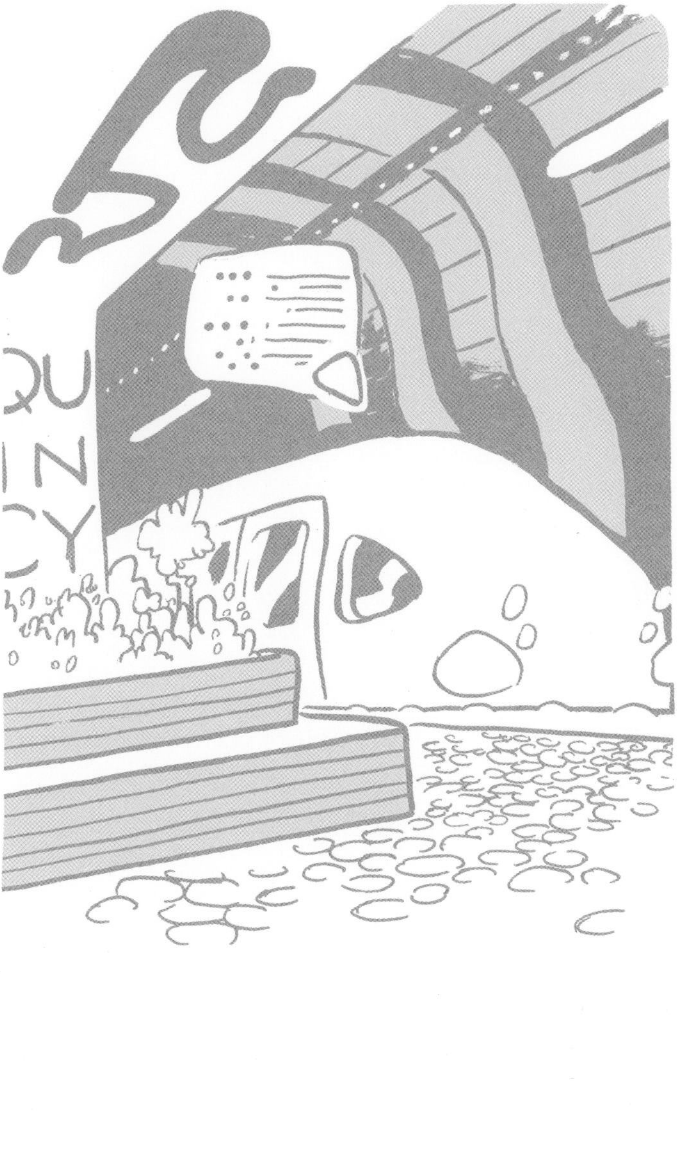
QU
IN
CY

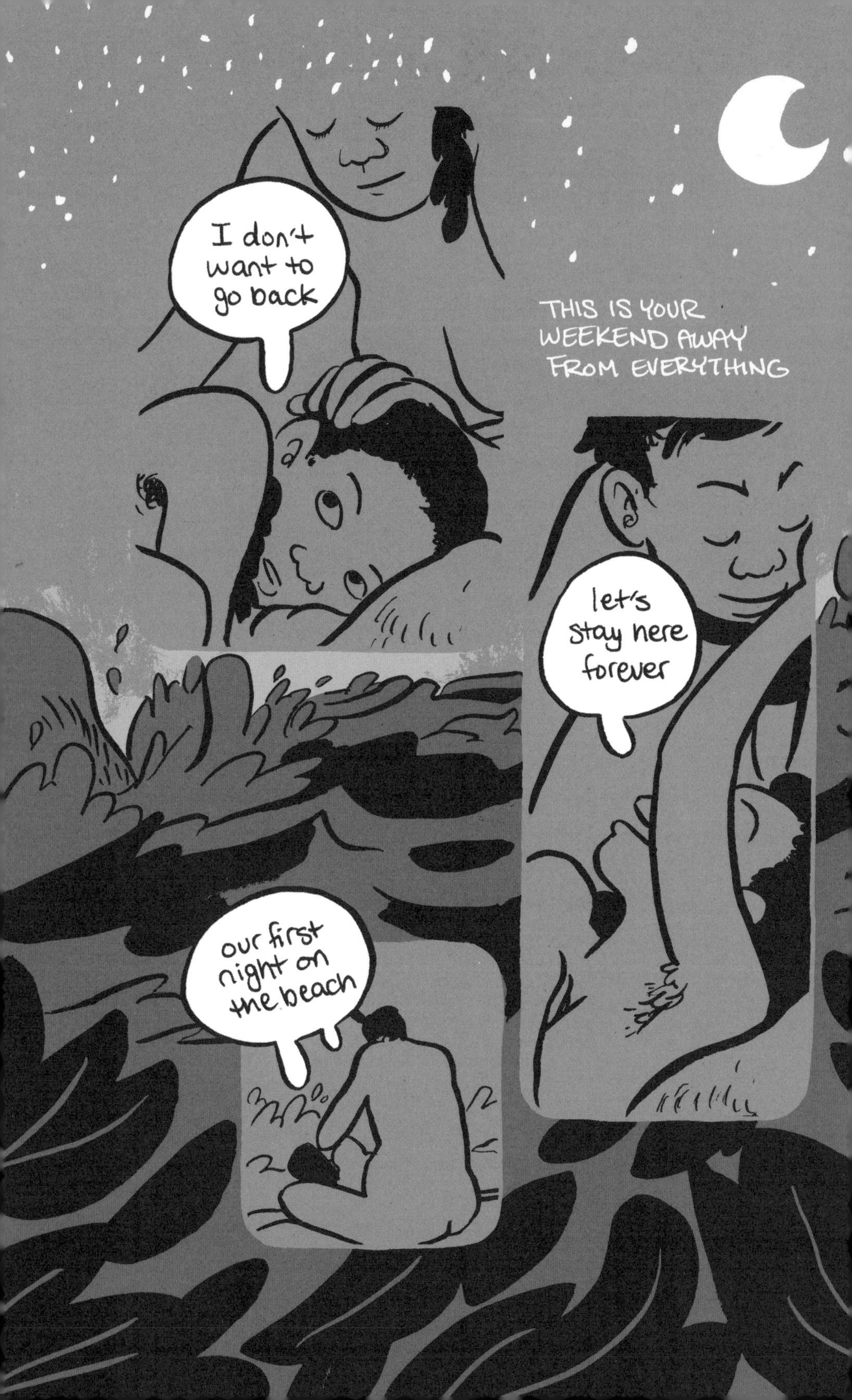
I don't want to go back
THIS IS YOUR WEEKEND AWAY FROM EVERYTHING
let's stay here forever
our first night on the beach

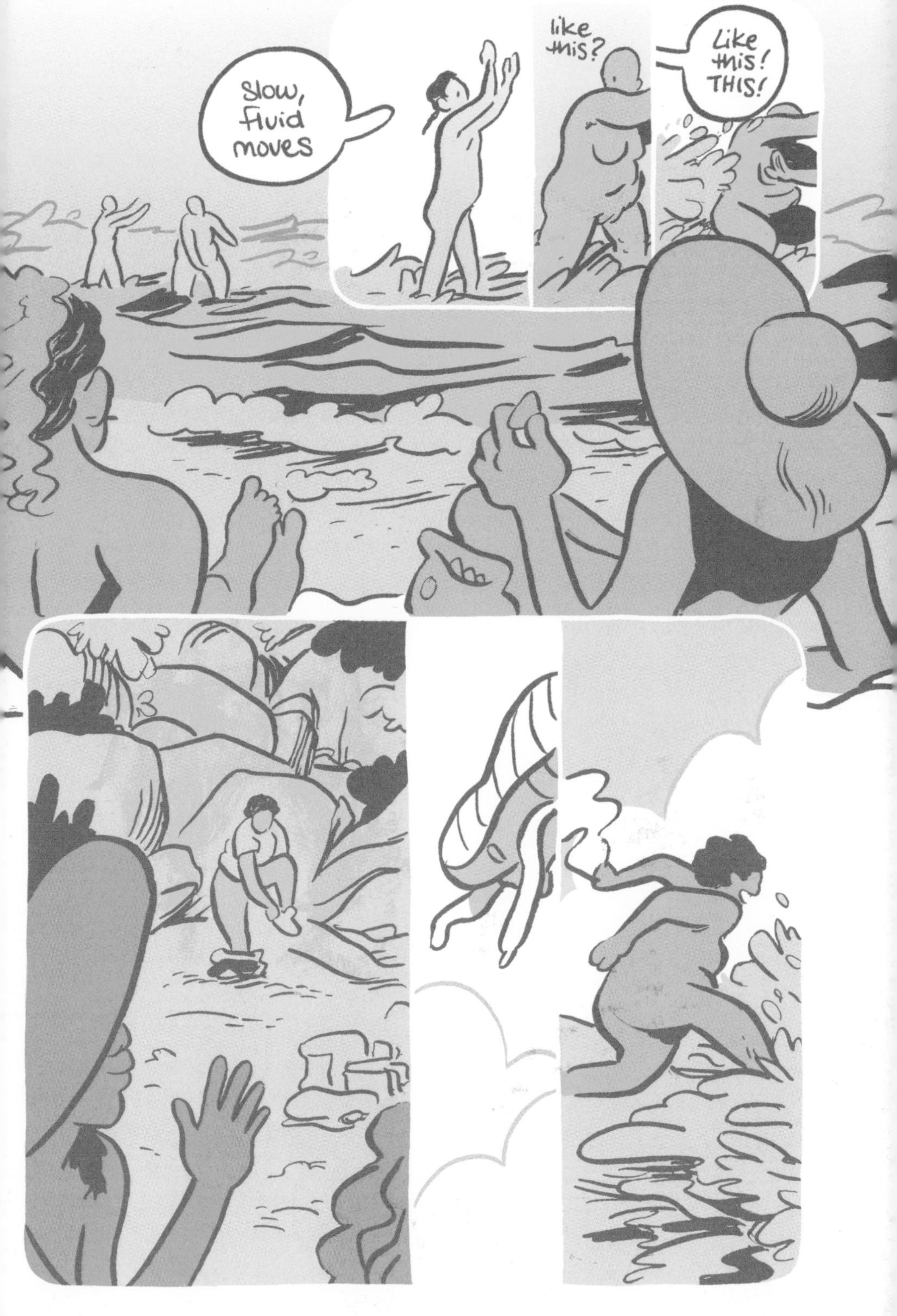
Slow, fluid moves
like this?
Like this! THIS!

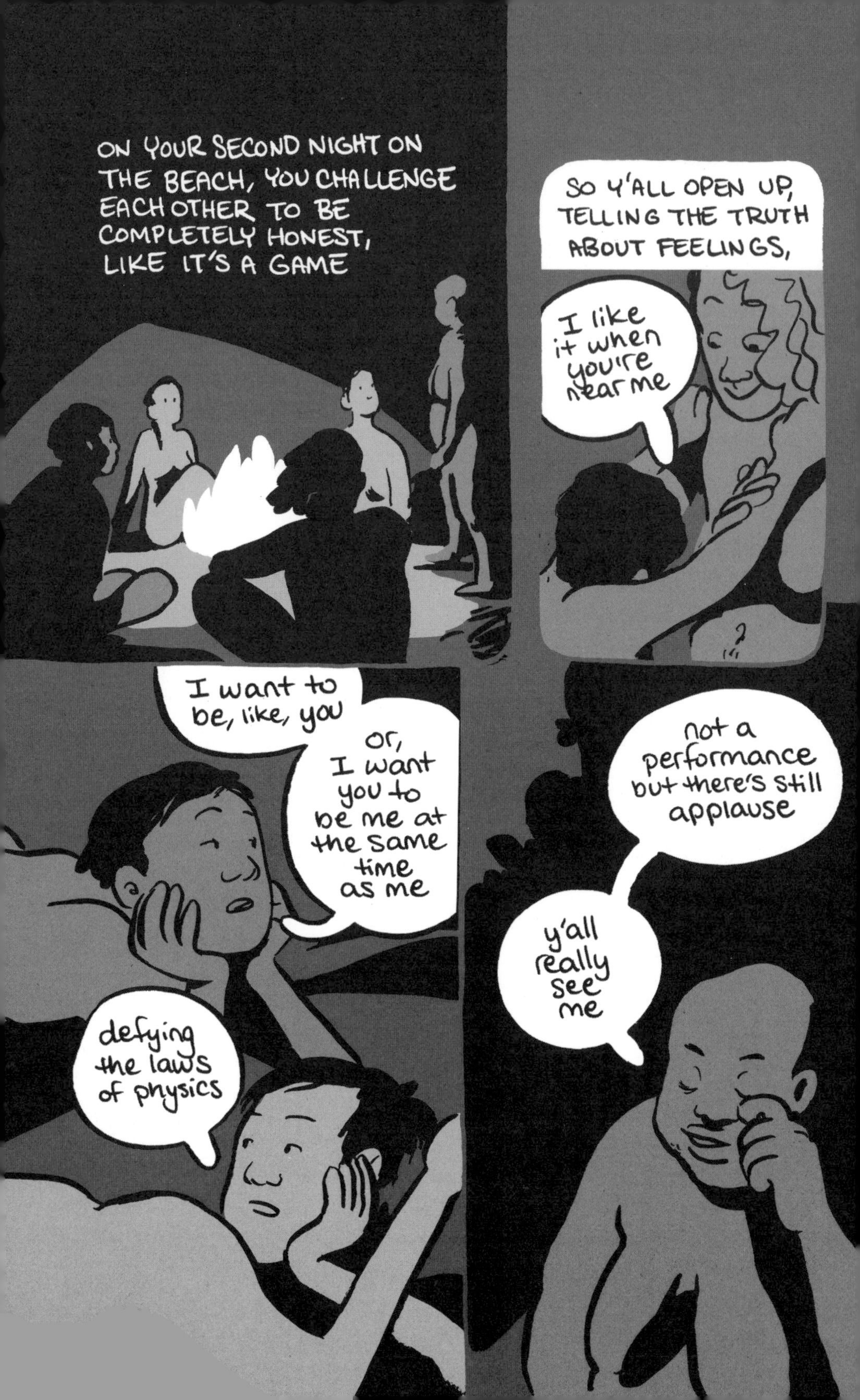
ON YOUR SECOND NIGHT ON THE BEACH, YOU CHALLENGE EACH OTHER TO BE COMPLETELY HONEST, LIKE IT'S A GAME
SO Y'ALL OPEN UP, TELLING THE TRUTH ABOUT FEELINGS,
I like it when you're near me
I want to be, like, you
or, I want you to be me at the same time as me
defying the laws of physics
not a performance but there's still applause
y'all really see me

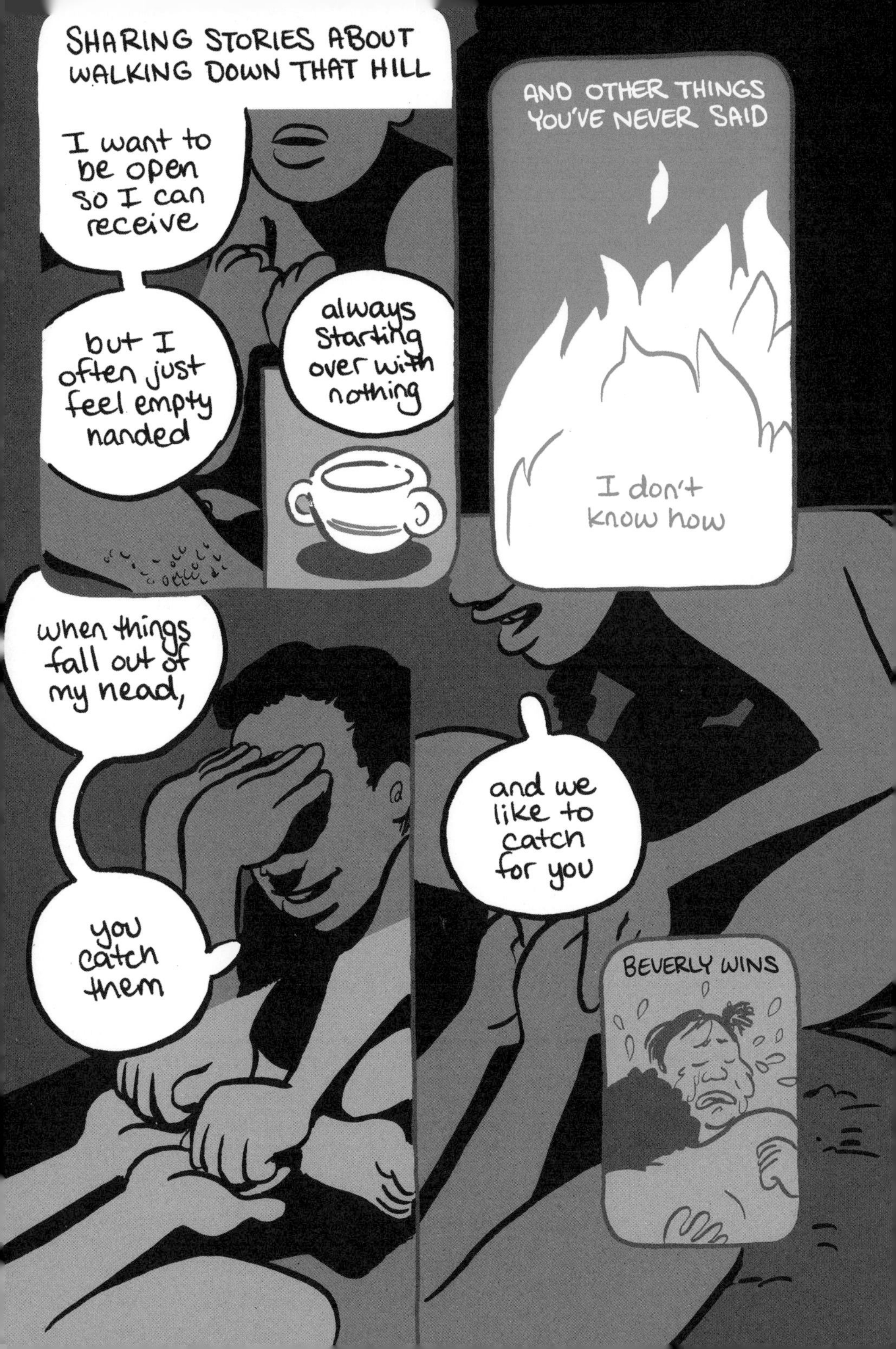
SHARING STORIES ABOUT WALKING DOWN THAT HILL
I want to be open so I can receive
but I often just feel empty handed
always starting over with nothing
AND OTHER THINGS YOU'VE NEVER SAID
I don't know how
when things fall out of my head,
you catch them
and we like to catch for you
BEVERLY WINS

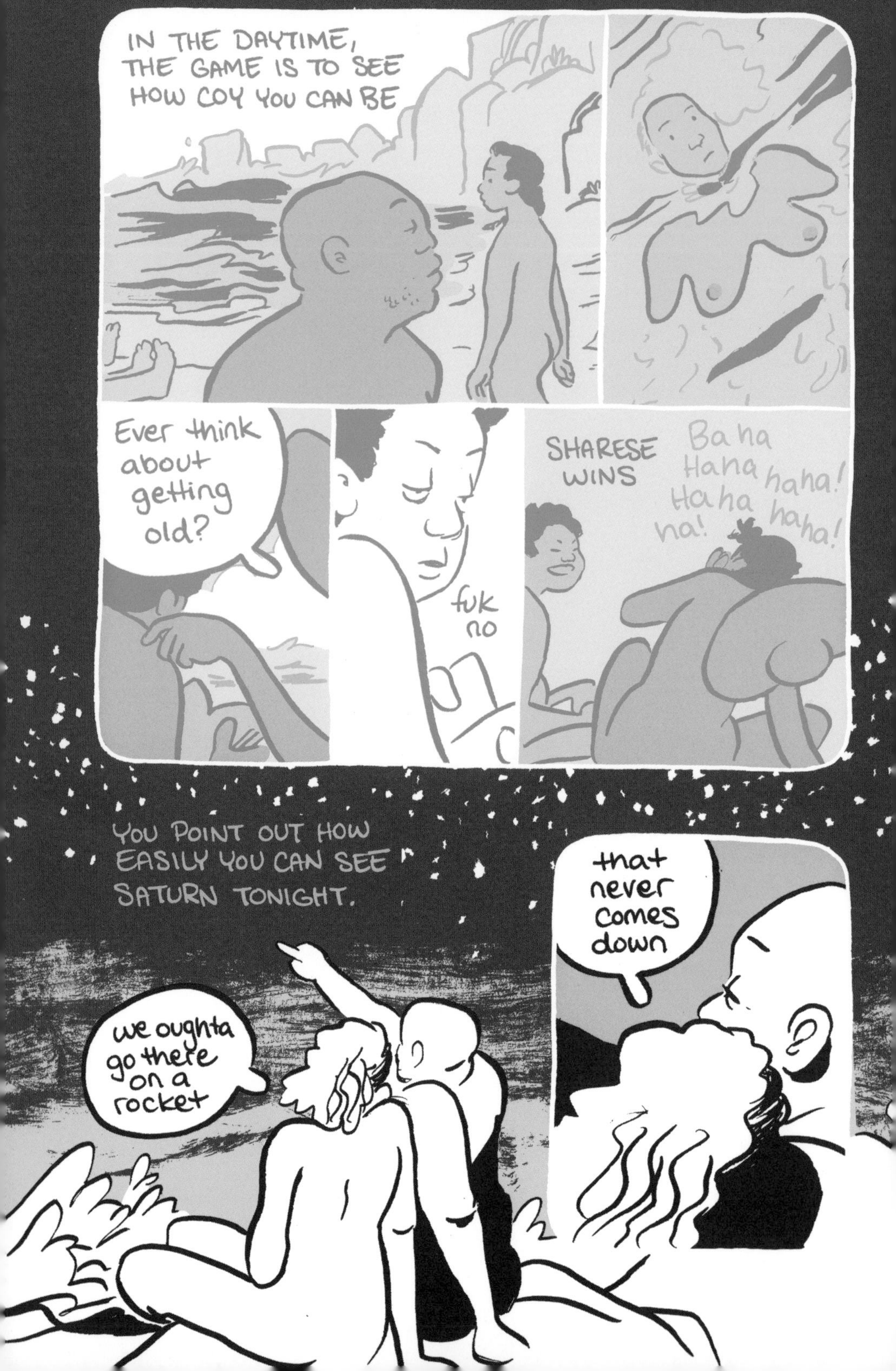
IN THE DAYTIME, THE GAME IS TO SEE HOW COY YOU CAN BE
Ever think about getting old?
fuk no
SHARESE WINS
Ba ha Hana haha! Ha ha haha! na!
YOU POINT OUT HOW EASILY YOU CAN SEE SATURN TONIGHT.
we oughta go there on a rocket
that never comes down

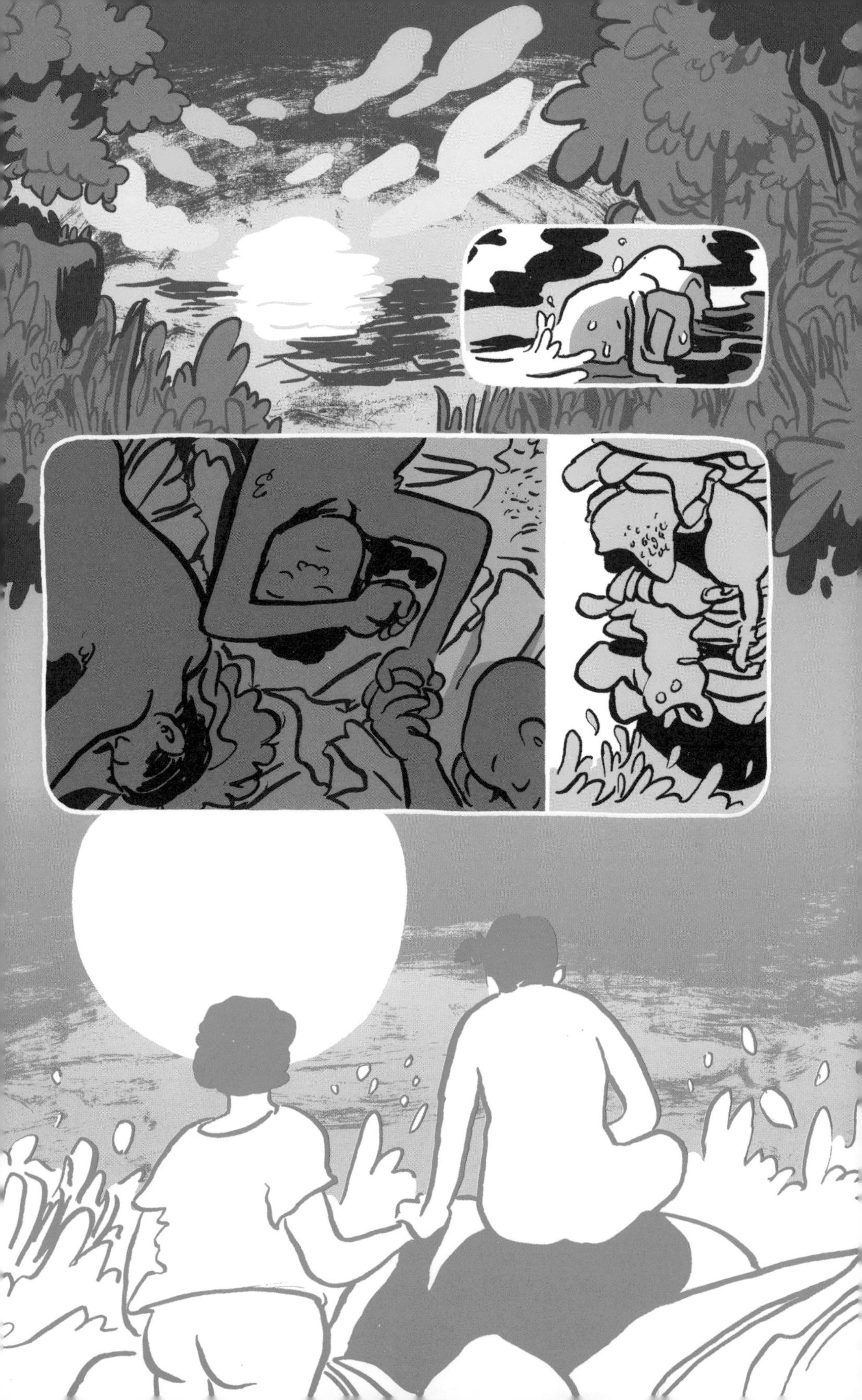

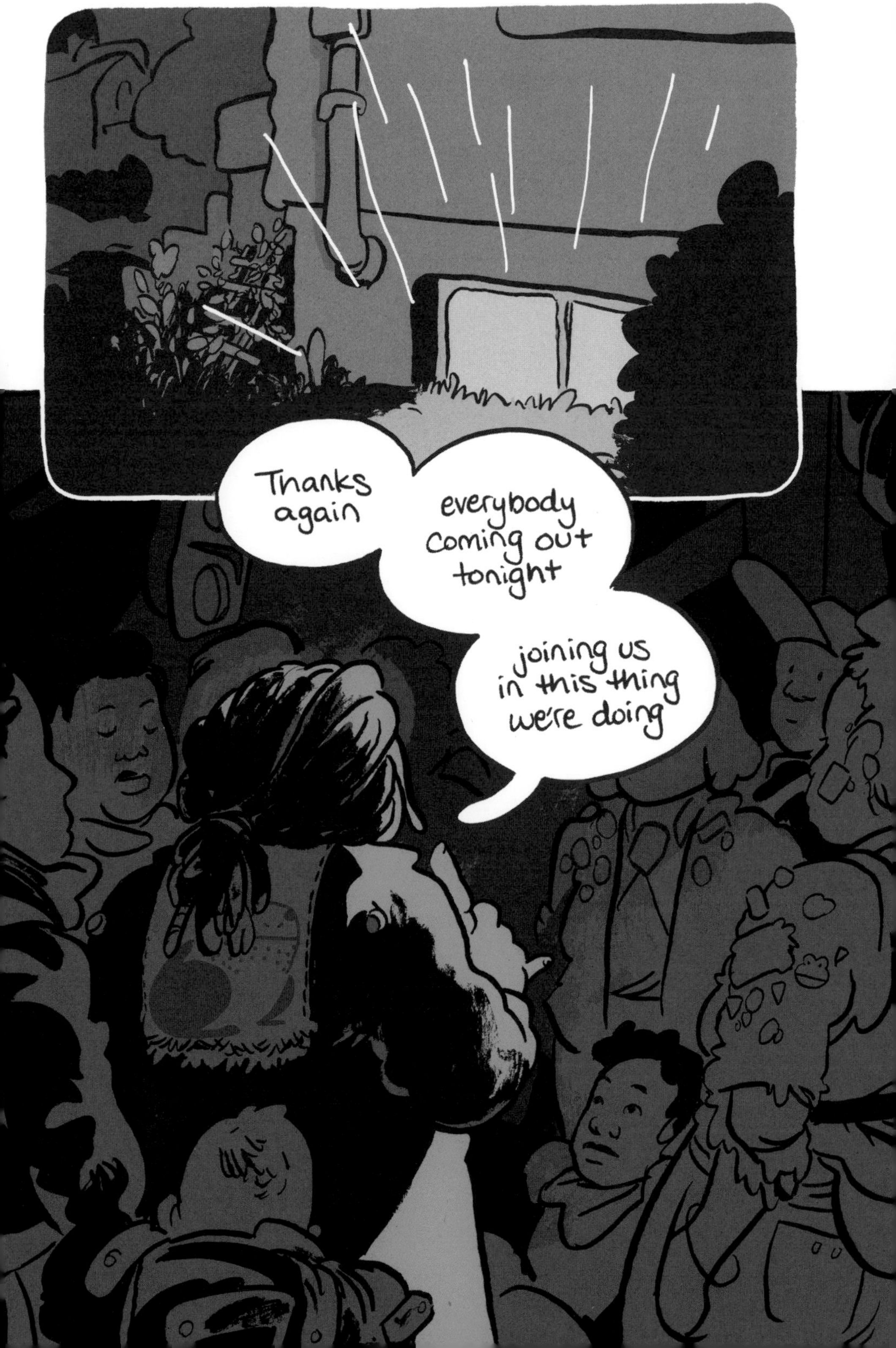
Thanks again
everybody coming out tonight
joining us in this thing we're doing

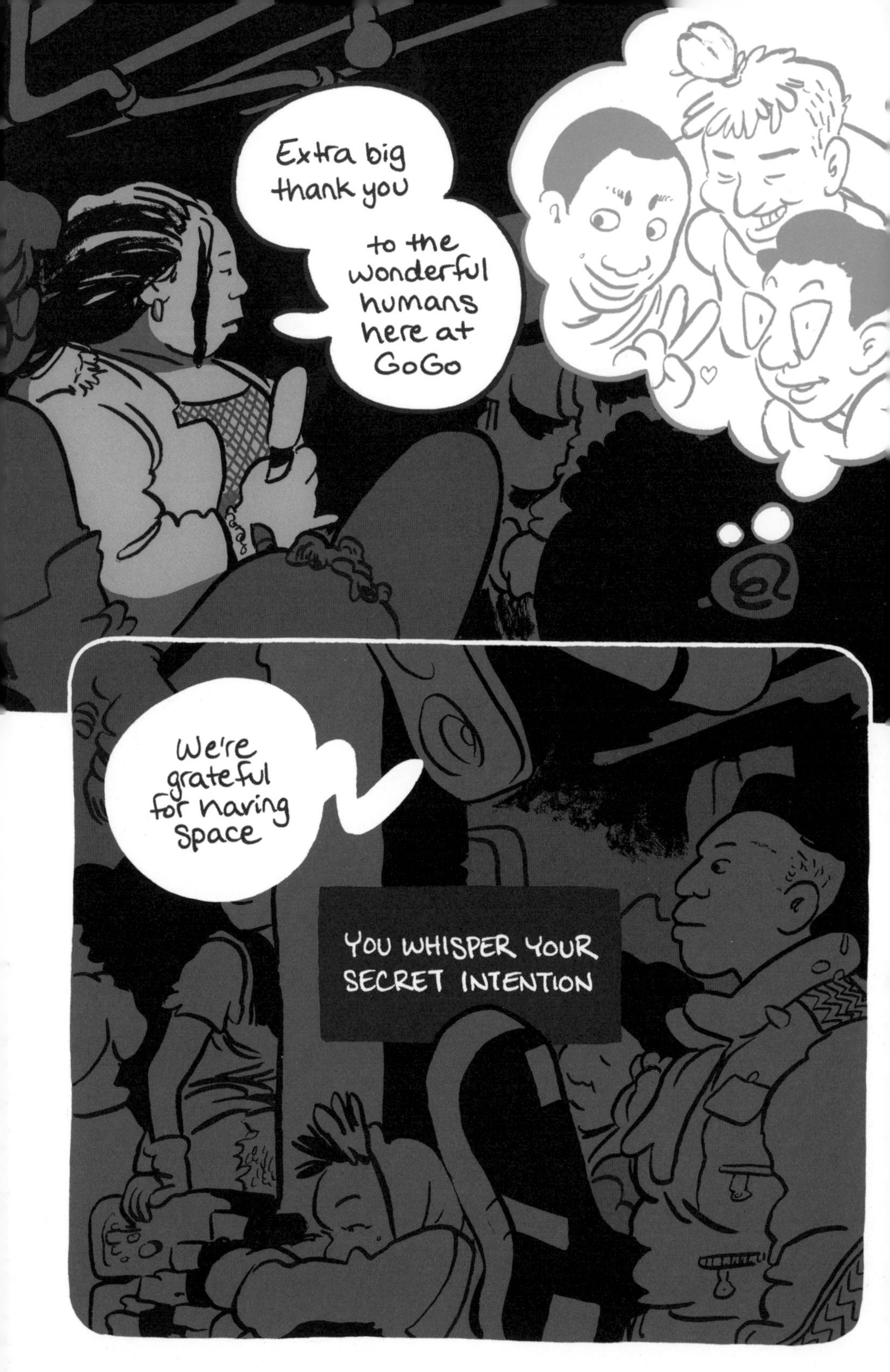

Extra big thank you
to the wonderful humans here at GoGo
We're grateful for having space
YOU WHISPER YOUR SECRET INTENTION

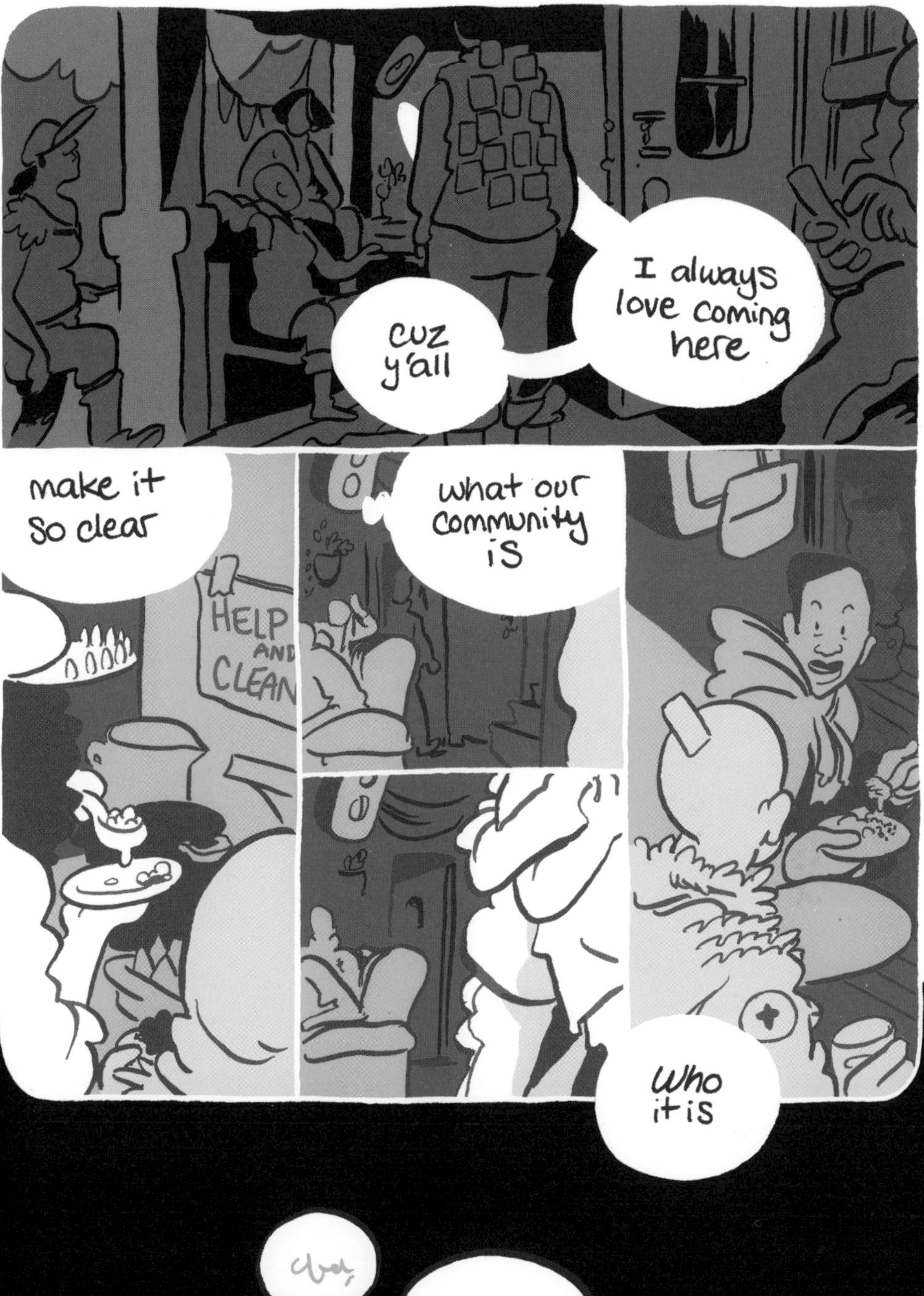
I always love coming here
cuz y'all
make it so clear
HELP AND CLEAN
what our community is
Who it is
I know, right?

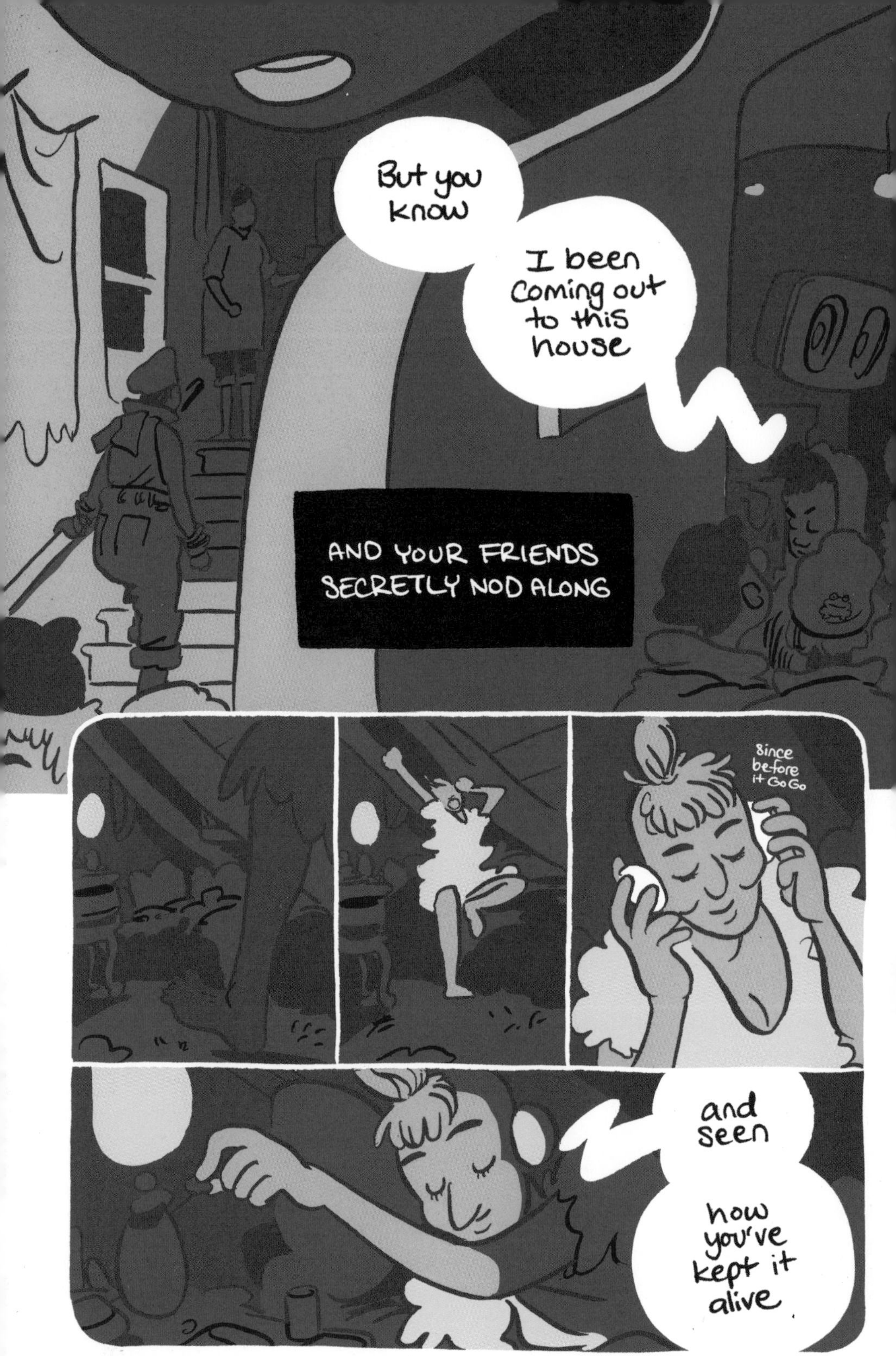
But you know
I been coming out to this house
AND YOUR FRIENDS SECRETLY NOD ALONG
since before it Go Go
and seen
how you've kept it alive

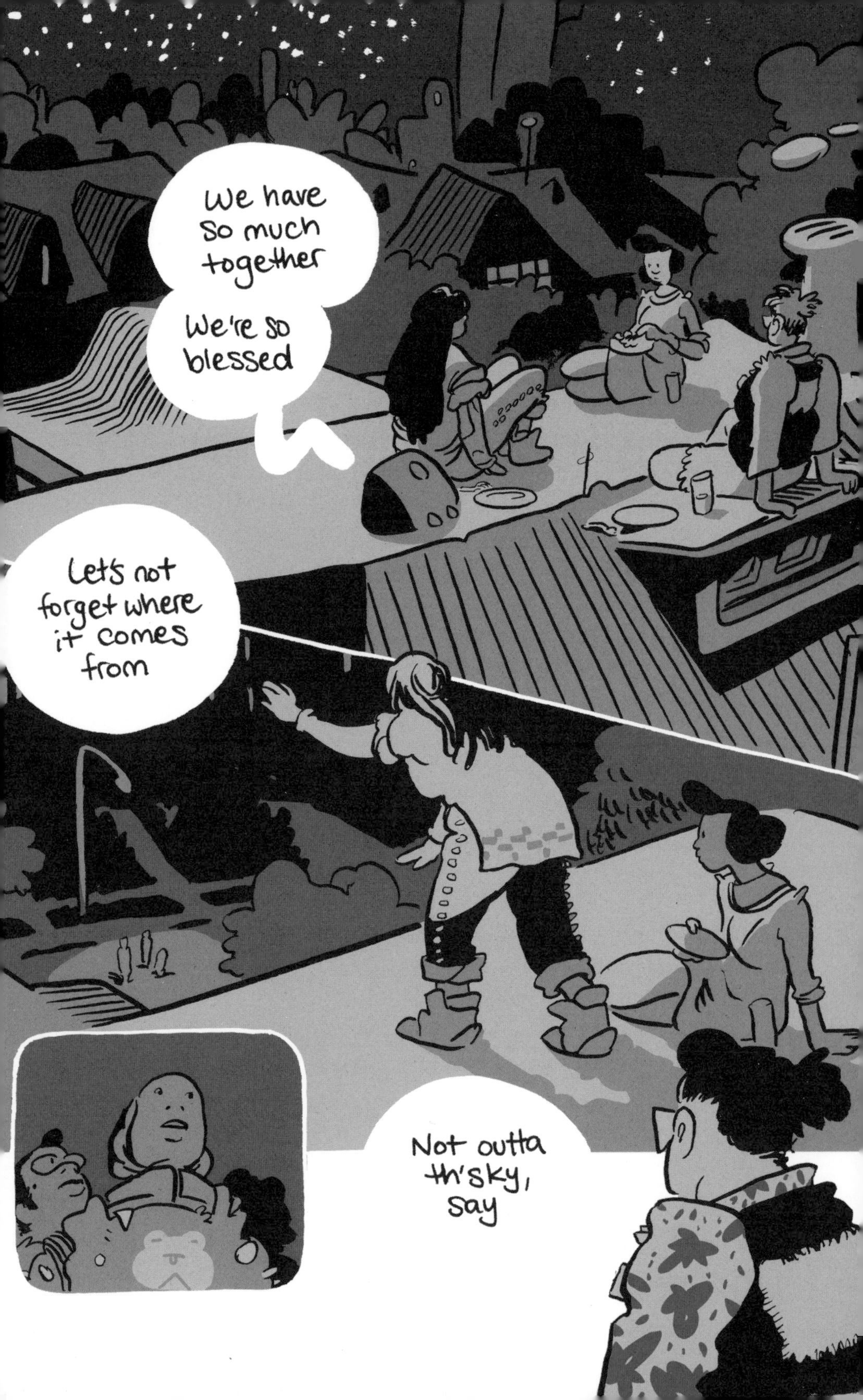
We have so much together
We're so blessed
Let's not forget where it comes from
Not outta th'sky, say

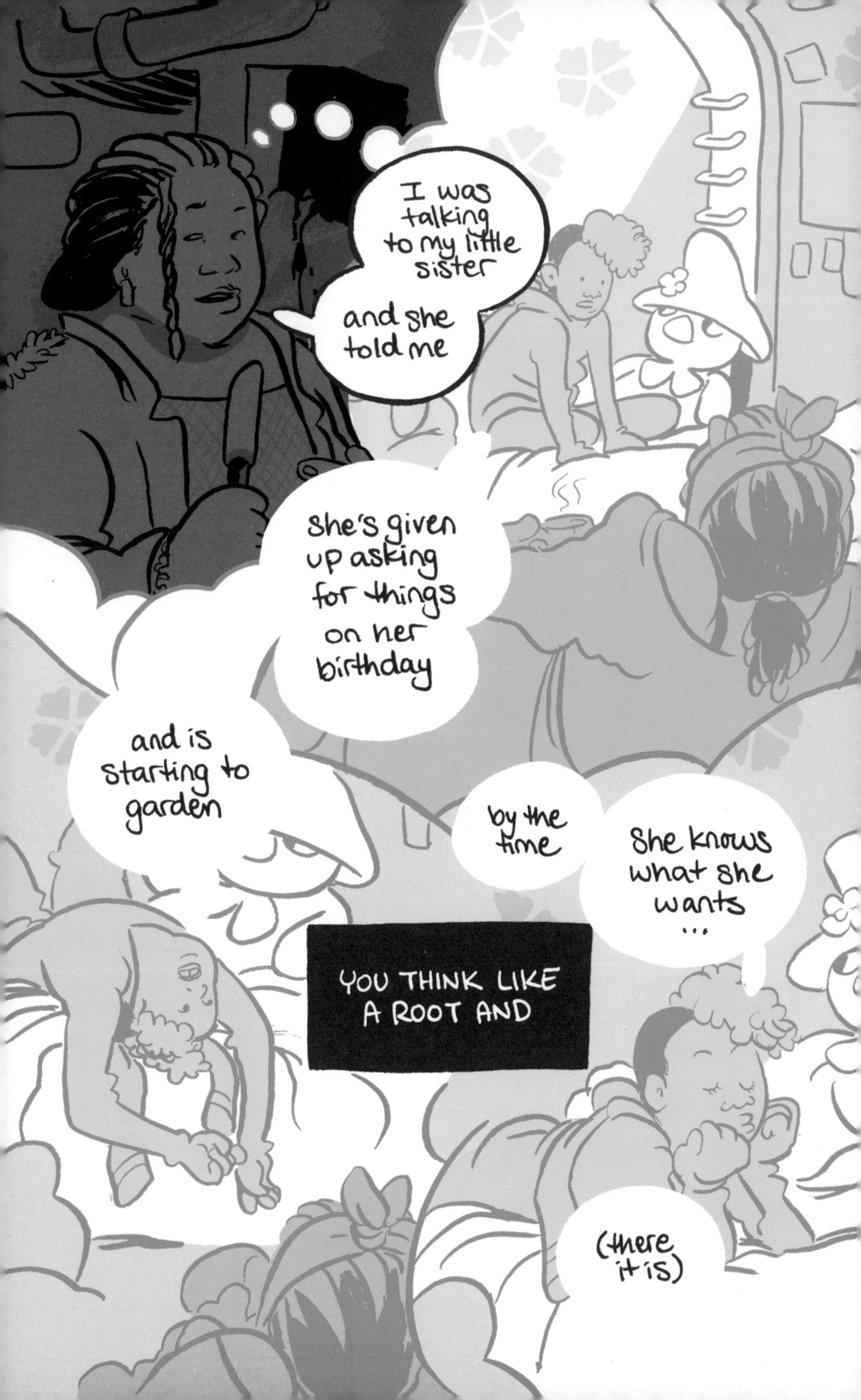
I was talking to my little sister
and she told me
she's given up asking for things on her birthday
and is starting to garden
by the time
She knows what she wants ...
YOU THINK LIKE A ROOT AND
(there it is)

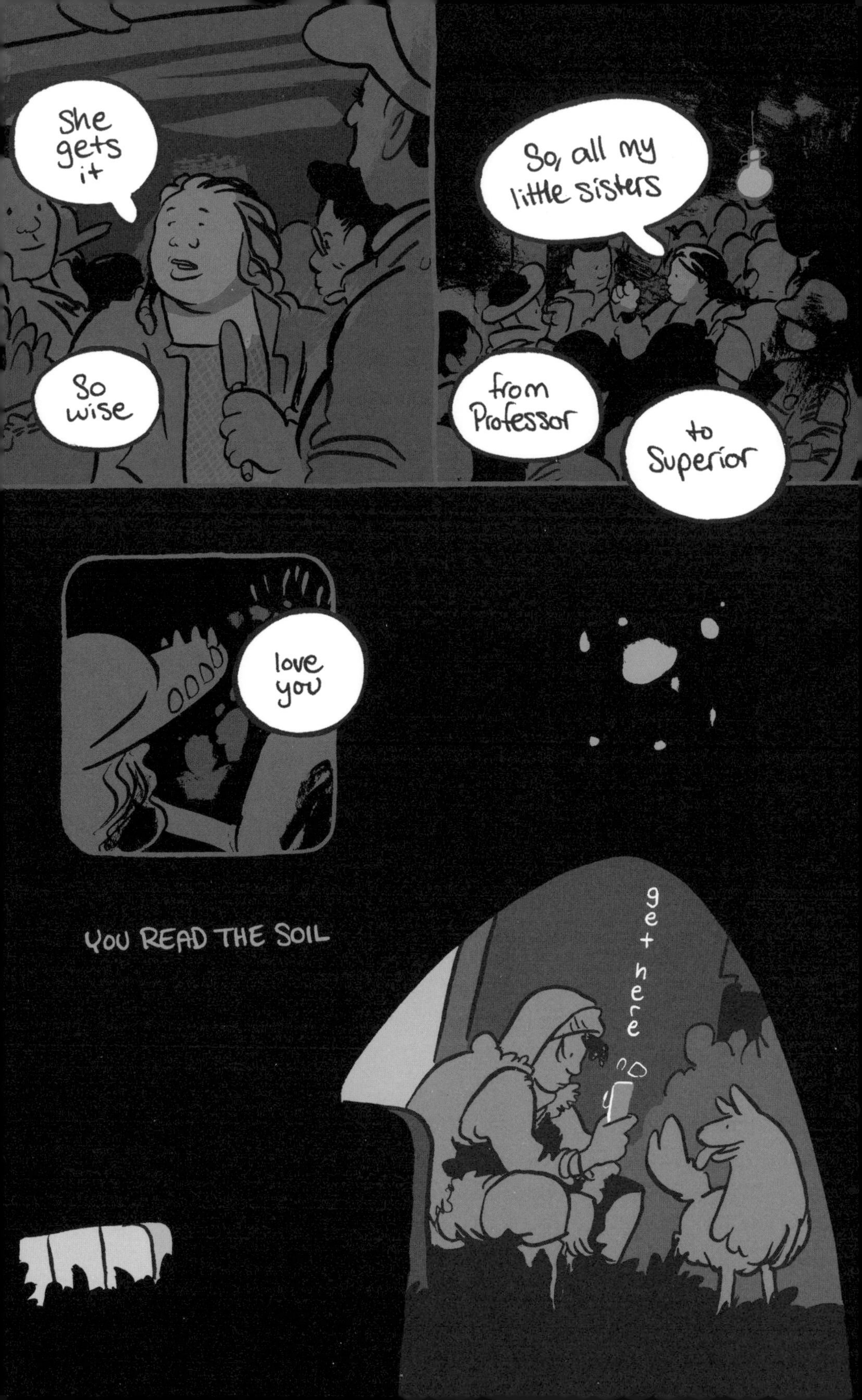
She gets it
So wise
So, all my little sisters
from Professor
to Superior
love you
YOU READ THE SOIL
get here

KEVIN CZAP (PRONOUNCED "CHAP") WAS RAISED IN N. VA, STUDIED ART IN CLEVELAND, AND IS NOW BASED IN PROVIDENCE, RI. THEY RUN THE MICROPRESS CZAP BOOKS, ENDEARINGLY REFERRED TO AS "COMICS MOM." IN 2016, CZAP RECEIVED THE 2ND ANNUAL CARTOON CROSSROADS COLUMBUS (CXC) EMERGING TALENT AWARD FOR THEIR WORK AND INVOLVEMENT IN THE COMICS COMMUNITY.

THIS COULDN'T HAVE BEEN MADE WITHOUT

CATHY, LIZ, MATT, MOM AND DAD, O, JOHN, DAG HOUSE, MATT AT PERFECTLY ACCEPTABLE, ANNIE, CZAP BOOKS FAM, & TOM AND JORDAN AT UNCIVILIZED BOOKS

AND UNENDING LOVE & THANKS TO

NICK KRATSAS, JUSTIN DAVEY, JESS WHEELOCK, VIRGINIA PAINE, HECTOR SILVA, L NICHOLS, VICTORIA RUIZ, MAREN JENSEN, VEGA XEROX, EVERYONE AT GIRL CONGRESS, JON WOLFE, RYAN SANDS, JOSH BURGGRAF, ELEANOR DAVIS, GEORGIA WEBBER, SOPHIA FOSTER-DIMINO, DARRYL AYO, JEREMY SORESE, SOPHIE YANOW, KATRINA S. CLARK, MEREDITH GRAVES, CMOV, BRIANNA DEAREST, AMBER DEAREST / FULL HOMO, LAURA AND TESS BROWN-LAVOIE, CXC, RA WASHINGTON / GUIDE TO KULTUR, LYNN RODEMANN, KRISTEN WARD, STEPHEN FLOYD, KATE SCHAPIRA, AIMEE FLECK, NOW THAT'S CLASS, MOSH EISLEY, VVK, LEGION OF DOOM, HOAX ZINE, DYKE NIGHT AT AURORA, STONECOLD BIKINI ON WRUW, GALACTIC RABBIT, JONI MITCHELL, TIM GUNN, AND THE WNBA

RECORDED IN CLEVELAND, OH, WITH ADDITIONAL WORK DONE IN PROVIDENCE, OAKLAND, SEATTLE, AND RENO

REMIXED AND MASTERED AT GIRL CONGRESS IN PROVIDENCE, RI

UNCIVILIZEDBOOKS.COM